Management
Issues in
Social Services

Management Issues in Social Services

Editor

S Vasoo

National University of Singapore, Singapore

W⊖ World Scientific

NEW JERSEY · LONDON · SINGAPORE · BEIJING · SHANGHAI · TAIPEI · CHENNAI

Published by

World Scientific Publishing Co. Pte. Ltd.

5 Toh Tuck Link, Singapore 596224

USA office: 27 Warren Street, Suite 401-402, Hackensack, NJ 07601

UK office: 57 Shelton Street, Covent Garden, London WC2H 9HE

Library of Congress Cataloging-in-Publication Data
Names: Vasoo, S. editor
Title: Management issues in social services / editor, S. Vasoo, National
    University of Singapore, Singapore.
Description: New Jersey : World Scientific, [2026] | Includes bibliographical references and index.
Identifiers: LCCN 2025020921 | ISBN 9789819815029 hardcover |
    ISBN 9789819815036 ebook | ISBN 9789819815043 ebook other
Subjects: LCSH: Social work administration | Social service
Classification: LCC HV41 .M2754 2025 | DDC 361.0068--dc23/eng/20250723
LC record available at https://lccn.loc.gov/2025020921

British Library Cataloguing-in-Publication Data
A catalogue record for this book is available from the British Library.

For any available supplementary material, please visit
https://www.worldscientific.com/worldscibooks/10.1142/14362#t=suppl

Desk Editors: Soundararajan Raghuraman/Yulin Jiang

Typeset by Stallion Press
Email: enquiries@stallionpress.com

Preface

The Department of Social Work at the National University of Singapore's (NUS) Faculty of Arts and Social Sciences hosted the Social Service Leaders Exchange Programme (SSLEP). The exchange programme, which aims to promote philanthropy and social development, was established by the Ee Peng Liang Memorial Fund and supported by local philanthropic groups. This monograph is collated from the various workshop discussions undertaken by the various groups of social service leaders who were participants and from contributions of articles by some scholar-practitioners.

The two-week programme saw selected social workers and social service leaders from Asia, in particular ASEAN, attending workshops to learn about and participate in sharing their experiences in their own communities with Singapore social work and service practitioners. The programme promotes a discussion of issues faced by social workers and service practitioners in Singapore and the region and facilitates exchanges of ideas on social challenges and responses across Asia.

The management of social services has not attracted much interest as this is always seen as non-profit activities and a charitable cause. However, over the years this service sector has expanded and requires good management skills to make the delivery of service more cost efficient, effective, and accountable.

The management of social services requires an in-depth understanding of various social issues and problems faced by residents and clients in need of help and those who are vulnerable to social difficulties. There are also people who lack the capabilities and knowledge to seek help when needed. Therefore, those in the management of social agencies must be able to analyze the varying reasons related to the barriers in preventing people in need to get access to services which are helpful to them. Importantly, management must find ways to make social agencies more accessible to those in need.

This monograph on management issues in social services is compiled from leadership workshops conducted and contributions of articles submitted on some key management issues facing social service leaders. Some of these management issues were brought up for them to follow through in managing their respective organizations. Ideas about making social services more responsive to those clients the social agencies vouch to serve and to prepare the agencies in meeting new emerging social problems facing the community.

About the Editor

S. Vasoo completed his secondary education in 1959 and went to work for six years to support his family. Thereafter, he passed the university entrance examination and enrolled as a mature student at the then Singapore University. Dr. Vasoo obtained his Diploma in Social Studies with distinction. He pursued further studies and graduated from the University of Hong Kong with a Master's degree in Social Work in 1974 and a Doctorate in 1985. He was awarded the Jean Robertson Book prize for his outstanding performance in the Social Work Master's course. He was also awarded the Social Work Alumni Award by the NUS Department of Social Work and the Distinguished Alumni Awards by the Faculty of Social Science of Hong Kong University and the National University of Singapore. Dr. Vasoo was awarded the Distinguished Volunteer Award by the Ministry of Social and Family Development in November 2024.

He taught as a lecturer at the Department of Social Studies, University of Singapore. He worked as a social worker and later as a social work administrator. He was appointed Executive Director of the Singapore Council of Social Services in the early 1980s. He was elected as a Member of Parliament in the Government of Singapore from 1984 to 2001. He also served as Chairman of the Government Parliamentary Committee for Community Development.

About the Contributors

Angelica Ang Ting Yi graduated from the National University of Singapore, majoring in Life Sciences and Public Health. She is interested in the health and environmental sciences, spanning an eclectic mix of topics such as conservation, environmental virology, and healthcare policy. During her undergraduate study, she was active in community service and has been keen to understand the outcomes of social service delivery to various client groups. She became interested to know how people given the assistance and support are coping with the assistance granted. In understanding the outcomes of help, agencies can then design more effective ways to reach out to the needy and assist them more effectively. These outcome issues motivated Angelica to work with experienced social scientists like Dr. Leong Chan-Hoong to explore areas of evaluation of social service outcomes and enable social agencies to be more competent in carrying out service evaluations. She has undertaken a few projects in these areas.

In her free time, Angelica enjoys watching arthouse films.

Ang Hao Yao actively leads a few local charities in Singapore. He is a private investor who is active in the charity sector and is currently the Chairman of Credit Counseling Singapore, a charity helping individuals and small businesses in debt distress. He also served as the Chairman of the National Kidney Foundation and is on the board of the charities Securities Investors Association (Singapore) and the SingHealth Fund. He was a former Chairman of SATA CommHealth and also serves on the Audit Committee of The Helping Hand.

Mr. Ang has worked in a few financial institutions and banks in the departments of consumer banking, private banking, and corporate banking. Mr. Ang holds Bachelor's degrees in Mathematics and Economics, an MBA in Finance and Investment, and is a CFA charter holder. Mr. Ang brings extensive experience from leading and serving numerous charity organizations.

Isabel Sim is actively involved in philanthropic activities. She is a known trainer and author, committed to helping charities be financially sustainable through good stewardship of funds. She was formerly appointed Senior Research Fellow, Department of Social Work, Faculty of Arts and Social Sciences, National University of Singapore, as well as Director (Projects), Centre for Social Development (Asia). She served as Head of Corporate Governance Practice, Centre for Governance, Institutions and Organisations (CGIO), and was Senior Lecturer, Department of Strategy and Policy, NUS Business School, from 2012 to 2014. She obtained her Ph.D. in Finance from the University of Western Australia in 2011. She edited a series of Accounting and Finance Handbooks for Charities, including Budgeting and Cash Flow Management, Fund Accounting for Charities, Full Cost Recovery for Charities, and Cost-Effective Audit for Charities. She was also one of the lead authors of *Accounting for Good*.

Leong Chan-Hoong, Ph.D., is currently a Senior Fellow and Head of the Social Cohesion Research Programme at the S. Rajaratnam School of International Studies, Nanyang Technological University, Singapore. Prior to this, he has held senior appointments in various academic institutions and in a global commercial advisory firm (Verian Group, formerly Kantar Public). He received a Ph.D. (Psychology) from Victoria University of Wellington, New Zealand (2006), and an M.Sc. degree in Statistics (2011) as well as Applied Geographic Information Systems (2019) from NUS. His research focuses on immigration, interracial relations, national narratives, and human–environment interactions. He has served as Consulting Editor of the *International Journal of Intercultural Relations* (IJIR 2013–2015), *Asian Journal of Social Psychology* (2018–2024), and *Equality, Diversity, and Inclusion: An International Journal* (2024–present). Chan-Hoong is listed as one of the most prolific and established authors for research in acculturation and intercultural relations. He is an advocate for intercultural engagement. He serves as a Council Member at the National Integration Council in the Ministry of Culture, Community, and Youth and in related community advisory boards on social integration.

Vincent Ng Chee Keong is currently the Dean of the School of Social Work and Social Development, Singapore University of Social Sciences. He completed his Ph.D. in Social Work at the National University of Singapore and has worked as a social worker in both public and medical settings. Under his steady and personable leadership, Allkin Singapore grew from three Family Service Centres in 2009 to a dynamic multi-service agency today, serving a diverse group of vulnerable populations.

Dr. Ng was a recipient of the Outstanding Social Worker Award (OSWA) in 2017. During his tenure at Allkin Singapore, he was instrumental in supporting four Promising Social Worker Award (PSWA) winners and one OSWA winner.

Vincent sits on several boards and committees to provide insights through the lens of a social worker. He currently serves on the Medi Fund Committee at the National Neuroscience Institute, Board of Visitors for Adult Disability Homes, Panel of Assessors on National Council on Problem Gambling, and National Council of Social Service's Leadership Selection Panel.

Dr. Vincent is actively involved in the training of the next generation of social workers to ensure that they have a balanced perspective, have their passions calibrated, and are equipped with relevant skills to be responsive to new social challenges.

Contents

Chapter 1

Conduct of Organizational Review: Challenges for Organizational Change and Development

S. Vasoo

Department of Social Work, National University of Singapore, Singapore

Introduction

The management of social services must be prepared for organizational review as organizations are often affected by changing social and demographic factors and they must be aware of the impact of these factors on their service delivery. Most importantly, there is a need for the key management leaders (this includes the board of directors, chief executive, and senior management staff) to undertake needs assessment surveys of the environment in which the organization operates so that actions can be taken to bring about changes and develop the organization.

In short, the management must take initiative to conduct a thorough organization review to cover data analysis and data management, including an evaluation of the impact on the service programmes delivered. In conducting organizational review, we must pay attention to corporate governance issues, particularly matters related to the interested party transactions. This chapter will cover some thoughts and processes on the conduct of organizational reviews and steps to implement changes and strengthen the organization. An organization's key management leaders may have to find innovative ways to go about conducting an organizational review and propose strategies to make their organizations robust.

Organizational Review and Preparedness

As a start, the key management leaders must size up the organization's social well-being. Like people, organizations have social health, which depends on the interest and commitment of the stakeholders, consisting of the board of directors, the management staff, major funders, the frontline workers, and consumers. To appreciate the social health status of the organization, an organizational review can be undertaken by assessing how all the stakeholders feel about their affiliation, levels of comfort in collaborating with one another, and the worthiness of being associated. If the organization is healthy, how does one know it is healthy? What are the indicators? The management leadership must identify indicators of organizational healthiness or wellness.

In assessing the social health of the organization, it will be possible to discover the factors contributing to poor organizational stability and poor organizational capacity.

When you have a good understanding of organizational health, then the key management leaders can begin to sort out the issues facing the organization.

Organizational Purpose and Energizing

Effective social service organizations have a clear sense of purpose, but this could be subverted by self-interested management leaders who are there for a name and a place to meet their own business agenda rather than helping deliver good services to reach out to as many needy people as possible. The primary purpose of the organization must remain steadfast, enabling the management leadership to have a clear focus to drive the organization ahead to fulfil its mission. The leadership must have people who really want change for the better and have the drive to move forward, despite facing various obstacles that could displace the organizational purpose. If we do not have management leaders who have the energy, then the organization will face resistance to change from within. Worse still, if the leaders are all lethargic, have no energy, and do not want to do anything, then there is little one can do unless there are a few leaders with tremendous energy. Consequently, the organization will wind up. To bring about organizational change, the leadership must encourage the participation of all. Those who lead must have the energy to do so and must generate the interest of all stakeholders.

Attributes and Profiles of Key Management Leaders

The attributes and profiles of key management leaders do affect the organization's efficacy and Effectiveness. Leaders with positive attributes who are behaviourally proactive, people-centric, and development-oriented will make the organization more sustainable and versatile in responding to social and community problems. Therefore, it is crucial for organizations to recruit socially initiative-taking and conscionable persons into management leadership.

To enable the organization to be more robust, it is important that key management leaders have *good interpersonal effectiveness*. Key management leaders such as the board of directors, chief executive, and senior staff who are assigned to bring about and inspire change should have good people skills and must be prepared to work with all others associated with the organization. Another attribute is that the key leaders must have positive human values and can interact appropriately and comfortably with all those involved. In addition, the key leaders must be able to communicate effectively and have a positive self-image. They should possess a good Emotional Quotient (EQ). However, the organization may have among its rank leaders with a high IQ but poor EQ who can resist being mobilized and do not support organizational change.

Another attribute that key leaders must have is the *public relations ability* to sell, market, and encourage people to clearly understand the rationale for organizational change. Long-winded stories should not be narrated as people become tired of hearing the same narratives. When people are ignorant or ill-informed of their stakes, they are unlikely to participate in organizational change.

An important attribute the key leaders should have is the commitment to achieve the organization's goals and the drive to accomplish them within a specified period; such commitment must be felt by all stakeholders. Without leadership commitment, organizational problems will not be solved. Key leaders must have the drive and not have a mindset trapped in the past and stuck in indecision. Such a mindset is not constructive and can be very destructive. Therefore, key leaders must control issues that are unfolding and manage them as they unfold.

Among the attributes the key management leaders must possess is good *organizing abilities*, which include communicating, mobilizing, analyzing, resourcing, and evaluating. All these abilities are applied to initiating organizational change.

There are four behaviour profile types of key management leaders in any organization. The first behaviour type is the go-go leaders who rush to do things on the go. The go-go leaders are doers and are helpful to the organization. They add value to the organizational set-up. The second behaviour profile type is the go-slow leaders. They tend to be cautious and take time to act. Some organizations may have go-slow types, and these leaders can make the organization conservative in its orientation. The third behaviour profile type is the slow-slow leaders who tend to take their own time to decide and act. Hesitancy in decision-making can hamper an organization's ability to respond. Finally, the last behaviour profile type is the no-go leaders who are indeed cautious and do not want to make any decisions at all. They must be pushed to move and undertake decisions.

These varying profile types of people in the organization, include key management staff, stakeholders, and the board of directors. These are the behaviour profile types one must work with to bring organizational change and development. Therefore, if the organization has many go-go people and a few go-slow people, then the go-go type can inspire others. If one has all the slow-slow type and the no-go type, then the organization may have to close shop ultimately or it will continue but move slowly. More often than not, there is still potential to bring about organizational change with a good mix of the go-go and go-slow types. They can effect change, but change may be quicker in some cases and may take some time in some other cases. Therefore, key leaders must feel that there are new possibilities for the organization to do better. Key management leaders must explore and address the new possibilities for organizational change. Key management leaders must bear in mind that they are accountable for improving the organization's service delivery. The opportunity to set up new outfits can help the organization grow. Those in key management leadership must have the energy to do so and must generate interest in the organization and seek answers to the specific issues facing the organization.

Approaches to Organizational and Programme Review

The approach that key management leaders to must undertake to conduct an organizational review exercise must be objective and enabling change. Various approaches and methods can be utilized, and these will be presented in this section. The outcome of such exercises can help the organization plan and implement relevant programmes that will meet the various needs of consumers. The organization is encouraged to undertake programme review exercises by key management leaders in varied small groups to produce suggestions and proposals.

Prior to discussing the various approaches and methods to conduct the organization review, it will be a good start for key management leaders to have a picture or vision for the future direction of their organization.

Analyzing Organizational Climate

Besides having the organization's vision, key management leaders can understand the *organization's climate, which is a combination of* stakeholders' feelings of wellness, safety, security, and being valued. The key management leaders in the organization care about all interested parties, do not treat them as objects, and are not utilitarian in their transactions. A positive climate is prevalent when the organizations are not only organization-centric but also people-centric. More importantly, key management leaders cannot forget or neglect the people who have a stake in the setup of the organization. Having supportive organizational factors such as caring key leaders, practicing fairness and, providing timely recognition can contribute to a positive organizational climate and thereby reinforce the feeling of ownership and comradeship. All these factors will help stakeholders be productive in moving the organization ahead and they will take responsibility for their tasks. The health of the organization is based on the total positive inputs by all who have a stake. At times, the organizational climate becomes unhealthy because key management leaders and other stakeholders blame one another and look for scapegoats.

Once the blame game is played, the organizational climate is not going to be positive. Therefore, the most important thing is to ensure that everybody in the organization has a part to play. All stakeholders have a place in the organization and are engaged in discharging their tasks. It will be counterintuitive to keep some stakeholders isolated and in the dark.

Developing Organization Vision

Key management leaders can examine if the organization has an established *vision which continues to be clear and contemporary*. The stakeholders in this case are the board of directors, senior management staff, main donors, and in particular consumers. All these stakeholders must have some ideas of the direction of the organization and whether the vision is still relevant in the light of changing environment and demographic needs.

There must be an affirmative consensus on steps to enhance the organization's image and ensure that it is people or consumer friendly, and the services are accessible to all those who need the support and assistance.

When undertaking the organizational review, a few practical approaches or methods can be applied by key management leaders, and these will be discussed. It must be borne in mind that each method or approach can be undertaken on its own, and there are indeed some limitations in fully diagnosing the issues, problems, and challenges faced. At times, a combination of methods and approaches can be adopted.

Applying the Focus Group Method

First, one can use *the focus group method*. In this situation, everybody comes together to share and identify what problems there are and then the people form smaller groups. Every group will come together, identify the problems facing the organization, the issues faced, and the challenges ahead. Several issues may come to the surface, members may be in conflict with each other, the organization might have no direction, it might have lost its sense of purpose, and there may be high attrition rates of staff and board members. When some or all these issues are solved, then the focus group will prioritize which issues are more pressing and problematic. Following this, the focus group will break into smaller sub-groups with each sub-group assigned to tackle a specific issue and come up with solutions. One must ensure that this does not turn into a complaint and griping forum.

Applying the Brainstorming Approach

The next method that can be applied is *the brainstorming approach*. In brainstorming, the key leaders can come together to examine and brainstorm on the various issues, problems, and challenges faced by the organization. The focus is to examine specific issues in depth and find workable solutions. In brainstorming, key leaders can vocalize their comments and offer opinions and ideas on the various issues, problems, and challenges faced by them and the organization. As the brainstorming group comprises key leaders, they can be considered biased unless they offer authentic feedback and views to make the organization better. Just to make the brainstorming sessions more useful and less biased, it will be more inclusive to bring in some shareholders including the major donors, community leaders, and the customers/consumers. The intention of this approach is to include a ground-up approach to mobilize people in the community and consumers or customers of the services to make the organization more community-oriented.

Applying the SWOT Analysis Approach

Next, key management leaders can undertake a *SWOT* (Strength, Weakness, Opportunity, and Threats) *analysis*. This can be a useful management tool for gaining insight into the robustness of the organization. Readers are encouraged to check the references and read about SWOT analysis. In applying SWOT analysis, it is critical to mobilize all key management leaders and the main shareholders to conduct the analysis based on the strengths, weaknesses, opportunities, and threats faced by the organization. Readers will acknowledge that all organizations have strengths. Some organizations have more weaknesses than strengths. Some other organizations do not see opportunities in the environment which is changing. There are new emerging needs such as the social neglect of the elderly, more child abuse in the community, an increase in human trafficking, wider class divides, and emerging mental health and workplace stresses. Key management leaders must plan for potential development in areas such as employment, setting up social enterprises, available new donors, and volunteers with skills and resources. All such opportunities can be tapped into.

Key management leaders can without fail identify the threats faced by the organization. The threats could be external threats, such as competition from other organizations which are coming into the same space and trying to take away their share of the organization's activities or consumers. There are also possibilities of threats from powerful influential persons who can subvert and prevent the organization from making progress.

These threats can be real or may be imagined threats, which can become real threats in the future. Another important key threat that key management leaders must take into thoughtful consideration is that funders may stop funding services. Overall, key management leaders should have contingency plans to deal with various other threats and opportunities.

Applying the Force Field Analysis Method

Another method that may be considered by key management leaders is to undertake *the force field analysis method*. To elaborate, this method postulates that in any social situation there are two forces acting against each other. One is the positive driving force that pushes the organization forward. Such a driving force is influenced by positive factors. In opposition is the restraining force which comprises factors that prevent the organization from moving forward. For example, if the organization has many funders, a lot of people with resources, a lot of skilled people with a high net worth, and many funded programmes, then the positive force will prevail, and the organization will be financially well endowed. The opposite is the restraining forces that make the organization financially unstainable due to the lack of funders, limited resources, and few high-net-worth individuals, and poor fund-raising projects.

It is posited that the organization with more restraining forces will not have a dedicated support network, capital, or resources, and leadership motivation. The presence of these negative forces will not be helpful. To bring organizational change, key management leaders must identify either the driving or restraining force, and reduce any negative forces. Actions must be implemented to increase the driving forces so as to increase the organization's capacity to change and develop.

To have a good grasp of the Force Field Analyses Method, one can study and appreciate the Force Field Theory by Kurt Lewin. One can use this as a tool for organizational review, change, and development.

Applying the Problem-Solving Approach

Finally, one can apply the *problem-solving approach*, which entails the group identifying the obstacle facing the organization. One can seek answers to the specific trouble facing the organization.

The approach will be to get members to form small groups and produce suggestions and solutions to the problems identified in the organization. The axiom is that for every problem there are solutions. At times, there is a need for a long-term or sustainable solution to the issue because problems keep recurring. The diverse groups of key management leaders will be required to participate in this approach.

Some Specific Strategies to Strengthen and Develop the Organization

Having gone through all the exercises that have been discussed earlier, key management leaders must focus on the findings of the organizational review and not pay lip service but act on them. A preliminary helpful step is exploring ways *to get* key management members to initiate various actions on the recommendations. In some organizations, some key management leaders tend not to act but talk only, the commonly used acronym for these leaders is "NATO." In this case, the organizations can have ideas, beautiful brochures, and ambitious plans but nothing is implemented. No action has been undertaken. However, with initiative-taking key management leaders, they will initiate programme-planning exercises.

Undertaking Programme Planning

The important thing is to get key management leaders to move into *programme planning*. The end objectives of any organization is increase the amount of funds raised, recruit more people who are skilful in social media and publicity, and reduce conflicts in the organization. By identifying the end objectives, the necessary means or steps to achieve the end can be planned. At times, leaders are caught in the ends and means muddling where the proper means to achieve the end itself are not justified. Other organizational issues follow the same process, and programme plans are to be implemented for organizational change and development.

Promoting Teamwork in the Organization

Key management leaders must promote teamwork. An effective organization has teamwork. The senior management staff, the board of directors, and major donors must work together and be assigned specific responsibilities and duties. Where needed, task groups can be formed to find ways to deliver better services for the clients, evaluate the impact of the services, and examine ways to enhance the organizational image. The formation of varied task groups to do different things can help the organization foster better teamwork. In short, the organization must attract committed individuals to create a sense of trust and ownership of the enterprise. All these human factors will minimize problems and facilitate the cooperation of members to work as a team. To create teamwork, there is a necessity to decentralize various tasks and responsibilities.

It is noted that in some organizations, a few people such as the chairperson, secretary, and treasurer take all the responsibilities and do everything. Such a practice creates centralized leadership, and the burdens are not shared across the key management leaders. When one does not distribute the responsibilities, the organization becomes pyramidal in hierarchy with a top-down type of decision-making which may not be healthy. It will be helpful to create a bottom-up participatory process as insights into issues on the ground are critical to organizational response. Organizations with a flatter structure can make decisions efficiently.

Broadening the Leadership Base

To strengthen the organization, it is essential for key management leaders to take steps to *broaden the leadership base of the organization*. Therefore, the management cannot depend on only one key leader to operate the setup. The consequence of such a situation will be organizational paralysis upon the loss of the chief. Also, when the doors of the organization are closed to renewal of leaders such a barrier can make reduce the versatility of the organization and consequently its growth and development can be stifled. This can be worse when the leadership is too centralized and dependent on a handful of key management leaders. The sentry gateway approach in leadership succession can be a disadvantage, especially when talented persons are not inducted into the organizational setup. It will be a pity if the prevailing key management leaders adopt a repulsive attitude to leadership renewal that might prevent revitalizing change and the development of the organization.

The answers to organizational leadership succession are complex. However, one pertinent action for key management leaders is to scout for and recruit different people with diverse abilities to volunteer and be assigned projects to strengthen the organization so that potential consumers who would not otherwise benefit from the services are positively impacted.

Another way to broaden the leadership base will be to recruit natural leaders or local leaders in the community where the organization is established. In addition, people with high net worth, those good in communication, and others with specialized skills such as IT, software, and social media skills can be enlisted. Such a broad range of talented volunteers can be groomed to be potential leaders of the organization.

Encourage Leadership Development

Another important task for the key management leaders is to ensure the *growth of leadership* in the organization. Grooming committed and capable individuals to accept leadership must be on the agenda of key management leaders who cannot count on one or two individuals to conduct the organizational tasks. Such an overreliance on a few leaders can stifle the broader involvement of others in sharing the leadership burden. Too much reliance on self-serving leadership or selfish leadership can in the longer term affect the sustainability of the organization. To encourage the development of leadership, the organization must be prepared to send potential new leaders to be trained in executive management schemes or courses. They can also be trained in interpersonal effectiveness and sensitivity training. By exposing the potential leaders to a variety of leadership training schemes, they will acquire the skills to improve the work of the organization.

Periodical Organizational Reviews

One essential organizational strategy that key management leaders can adopt is to conduct **organizational reviews** every two years involving the stakeholders coming together. Review exercise will assist in identifying or diagnosing the organizational health and /or the agency programme problems. Once the problems have been discerned, the key management leaders can find remedies to the various problems or obstacles. New ways to meet new challenging needs can also be identified.

Conducting Evaluation

Finally, one critical task that must be administered without fail by key management leaders is to conduct an *evaluation of numerous services or programmes delivered by the organization.* The organization has deployed resources to discharge diverse services or programmes. The outcomes of the services or programmes are based on assessing whether the programmes or services are cost effective and if the consumers are satisfied with them. The outcomes must be verified and the solutions that worked or did not must be assessed. The issues must be empirically evaluated. This is critical because all the ideas and solutions that are that are recommended will result in positive outcomes and hopefully contribute to organizational change. Where the outcomes are negative, the key management leaders have to take another look at the ways in which the indicators used in measuring the outcomes are relevant and dependable. Feedback from the evaluators and consumers of services or programmes is obtained to verify if the intervention is appropriate. The ultimate objective of the evaluation is that it should not be an academic exercise but an exercise to seek way to improve the organization's service delivery.

Besides evaluation efforts, the key management leaders must gather *feedback* from stakeholders. With the feedback, actions can be conducted to deliver organizational services effectively and efficiently. Feedback should not be put in the archives. When this happens, the consumers will become fed up with the minimal efforts made to deal with some issues and problems affecting them as well as the performance of the organization. Valuable feedback when implemented can improve the health of the organization, and stakeholders can take ownership and be prepared to find more resources to deliver the much-needed services.

Concluding Remarks

The key management leaders must be initiative-taking and committed to enabling the organization to respond positively to the social, environmental, and demographic changes, particularly in the case of Singapore, where 30% of the population will be above 65 years of age. The organization must be managed effectively and must be responsive to the inevitable changing social, psychological, and economic needs of the population, of whom a sizeable proportion will be ageing. Therefore, the organization must without doubt have on board good leaders who will actively conduct organizational reviews by applying various methods and/or approaches as discussed.

Certainly, good and open-minded people can be encouraged to accept key management leadership positions to drive the organization to grow and develop to provide services and support for community betterment. The leaders must have positive human values and dignity to serve without favour or expecting reward.

In conducting organizational change, the key management leaders must consider the timely implementation of much needed services for the consumers. This is important as wrong timing in intervention can create added complications for individual well-being. Otherwise, with serious displacement of purpose and misuse of funds, the organization might shut down if no other more enlightened leaders take over. Leaders who are change agents can sometimes ignore issues about the environment in which the organization operates. As can be witnessed, the environment is also changing; there is climate change, ecological change, demographic change, and now different pandemics affecting people and the leadership of the organization. The leadership of social service organizations should have or if not, acquire analytical skills to assess the changing social and ecological environment. Such capabilities of the leadership can enable the leaders to take initiative and actions to deliver relevant services for the client population the organization purports to serve. Having good analytical skills will make the leadership more adaptive, help strengthen social service delivery, and build a more resilient and viable organization which can be sustained through upcoming challenges.

Acknowledgements

S. Vasoo is indeed grateful to Ms. Yong Hui Hua, Project Executive of Social Service Leadership Program, Ee Peng Liang Memorial Fund, for helping to collate various information for this article.

Bibliography

Beckhard, R. and Harris, R.T. (1987). *Organizational Transitions: Managing Complex Change*, 2nd edn. MA: Addison-Wesley. Burke. WW.

Bloomerang. (2024). SWOT for non-profit. https://bloomerang.co/blog/how-nonprofits-can-use-a-swot-analysis.

Burnes, B. (2004). *Managing Change: A Strategic Approach to Organizational Dynamics*, 4th edn. Harlow: Prentice Hall.

By, R.T. (2005). Organizational change management: A critical review. *Journal of Change Management*, 5(4), 369–380.

Carnall, C.A. (2003). *Managing Change in Organizations*, 4th edn. Harlow: Prentice Hall.

Chron. (n.d.). Force field theory application. https://smallbusiness.chron.com/can-force-field-analysis-work-organization-5216.html.

Graetz, F. (2000). Strategic change leadership. *Management Decision*, 38(8), 550–562.

Grundy, T. (1993). *Managing Strategic Change*. London: Kogan Page.

Gummer, B. (1993). Organizational change. *Administration in Social Administration in Social Work*, 16(3–4), 205–214.

Hussain, S.T., *et al.* (2018). Kurt Lewin's change model: A critical review of the role of leadership and employee involvement in organizational change. *Journal of Innovation & Knowledge*, 3, 123–127.

Lewin. https://www.youtube.com/watch?v=64t_NIAG2QY.

Lewin's. https://www.youtube.com/watch?v=X9ujAtYAfqU.

Luecke, R. (2003). *Managing Change and Transition*. Boston, MA: Harvard Business School Press.

Mary, N.L. (2008). Transformational leadership in human service organizations. *Administration in Social Work*. http://www.tandfonline.com/loi/wasw20.

Reading, M.A. (2002). *Organization Change: Theory and Practice*. Thousand Oaks, CA: Sage.

Santhidran, S., Chandran, V.G.R., and Borromeo, J. (2013). Enabling organizational change – Leadership, commitment to change and the mediating role of change readiness. *Journal of Business Economics and Management*, 14(2). http://dx.doi.org/10.3846/16111699.2011.642083.

Senior, B. (2002). *Organizational Change*, 2nd edn. London: Prentice Hall.

Unrau, Y.A. and Coleman, H. (2006). Evaluating program outcomes as event histories. *Administration in Social Work*, 30(1). http://www.haworthpress.com/web/ASW.

Vasoo, S. (2023). *Singapore Ageing. Issues and Challenges*. Singapore: World Scientific.

Whelan-Berry, K.S. and Somerville, K.A. (June 2010). Linking change drivers and the organizational change process: A review and synthesis. *Journal of Change Management*. http://www.tandfonline.com/loi/rjcm20.

White, A., Wheelock, M., Canwell, A., and Smets, M. (2023). 6 key levers of a successful organizational transformation. In *Leadership and Followership in an Organizational Change Context*, pp. 197–218. IGI Global.

Wikipedia. (n.d.). Force-field analysis. https://en.wikipedia.org/wiki/Force-field_analysis.

YouTube. (2017). SWOT analysis of an NGO: SWOT approach. https://www.youtube.com/watch?v=2xquSq0MSAc.

Chapter 2

Data Management and Analysis in Social Service Sectors[*]

Leong Chan-Hoong and Angelica Ang Ting Yi

*S. Rajaratnam School of International Studies (RSIS),
Nanyang Technological University, Singapore*

Abstract

This chapter introduces how data from the social service sector can be obtained, managed, and analyzed. We first describe the different genres and classifications of databases and how they can be harnessed to make policy or program decisions. The types of data include information derived from ethnographic research, quantitative survey, primary vs. secondary databases, administrative data, and location-based information. Following this, we discuss the limitations of data management. It should be emphasized that this chapter is not aimed to demonstrate the full range of statistical models and data analytics but to give readers a flavour of the diverse possibilities in the field of data management and analysis, such that they may be more cognizant of the potential to harness reliable data from their current and future work.

---

[*]This chapter was originally published in L. Chan-Hoong and A. A. T. Yi (2021). Social Service Leadership Exchange Programme Lecture Series. NUS Department of Social Work.

Introduction

Singapore is a rapidly ageing society with a significant socio-economic disparity. The social service sector, with support from the state, offers ground-up initiatives and programs to aid vulnerable individuals and families. While this partnership underscores the spirit of collective reliance and social capital, there is nevertheless a need to ensure that the resources devoted to these community-based projects are utilized meaningfully and efficiently. This necessitates a procedural, systematic assessment of the inputs, outcomes, and other collateral changes. In other words, sound corporate governance and public accountability in the social service sectors are all but expected compliance.

To achieve this goal, social service agencies need to maintain and keep track of their financial accounts, and administrative records on the beneficiaries, and volunteers, management team, and the outcomes of programs, services, and/or new initiatives. Importantly, these data provide organizations with a compass for strategic planning and accountability. Specifically, which measure works and what do not? What is the social impact? Where are the gaps, if any? What is the opportunity cost? While these considerations determine social impact, the value of program evaluation, however, is contingent on the credibility and reliability of the methodology, data, and analytical techniques. The quality of these information matter as much to social service delivery. In summary, data management and analysis serve to meet a range of objectives; they include but are not limited to the following purposes:

Program evaluation

Social service agencies provide services to cater to the needs of their constituents. The outcome and impact of these activities, however, may not be evident and service gaps may arise due to blind spots or oversights. As such, an objective, evidence-based evaluation is necessary to help improve existing programs, plan new interventions, inform service gaps, and calibrate existing policies.

Accountability and justification

Social service agencies receive funding from state agencies and other philanthropic organizations to fulfil a mission. As such, there is a financial obligation to ensure that the resources are accountable and that the outcome of the program and spending are justifiable. It is a means to demonstrate to the stakeholders, donors, and community at large, on the areas where the resources they contributed had gone towards.

Types of Data

What are the different data types and sources? Due to the wide range of programs, services, and policies practised across the social service sector, different types of statistics are produced, each serving a different purpose, and with varying degree of reliability and validity. In other words, the data collected by any one agency is constrained by the genre of interventions, programs, or services. It is thus important to appreciate the cost/benefits, limitations, and efficacy of each dataset to make informed decisions on the type of data to collect. There are several ways by which we can classify the different types of data (Table 1).

Table 1.   Sources of Data.

Level of Data	Sources of Data	Representation	Data Analysis
Group level (secondary data)	**Census data** (e.g., age, income, gender, and residence location) **Government administrative records** (e.g., wealth, taxation, family structure, % of school attrition, delinquency, criminal records, criminal records, and election records) **Big data** (e.g., density and mobile phone location, tweets, bank transactions, search records, and Google Analytics) **Spatial data** (e.g., locations of amenities and geographical features)	Population	No inferential statistics needed
Individual level (primary data)	**Surveys/In-depth interviews** **Observer participants** **Focus group discussions** **Experimental designs** (e.g., pre- and post-intervention)	Sample	Inferential statistics needed, e.g., t-test

(i) Group-level data vs. individual-level data

One approach to the classification is based on group-level (i.e., secondary) vs. individual-level (i.e., primary) data types. Table 1 outlines the different characteristics and examples of the two levels of data.

There are two key differences between the group-level and individual-level data.

First, group-level data is representative of data at a larger, population-wide scale. On the other hand, individual-level data refers to data at a smaller scale and is only representative of individuals of the sample group from which data was collected from.

Second, when analyzing group-level data, there is no need for inferential statistic testing since data is already collected at the population level. However, when analyzing individual-level data, further inferential statistic testing (e.g., t-test) is often required. For instance, if there is a survey with a few hundred people (individual-level data) on an intervention program, you may need to conduct statistical testing on data collected from pre- and post-intervention groups to see if the differences are statistically significant.

However, as we go about collecting data to justify the programs our organizations have, in many cases, we do not just use one type of data. Instead, we may choose to use a mixed method design, whereby both group-level and individual-level data are utilized — for instance, in our evaluation, we could choose to have a survey, as well as look at census data.

(ii) Objective and subjective data

Apart from group-level and individual-level distinction, data can also be categorized into objective and subjective measurements. For objective indicators, information is very clear-cut and does not require further interpretation (e.g., financial expenses, observable activities, amount of time taken, and budget spent on housing rental). These are data that we can unanimously agree to be high or low, or good or bad. On the other hand, subjective data often requires some deliberation and interpretation (e.g., personal and user experiences) after it has been collected.

Observable behaviour and objective data tend to paint a more powerful portrait than evaluative, latent opinions. This is due to the fact that subjective data is prone to social desirability bias; that is, people provide an answer that will cast them in a positive light. For instance, in a question on volunteering for charitable causes, a respondent may be inclined to inflate his or her contribution to be seen as likeable by societal standards. This might lead to bias and inaccuracies in the data. Several examples of objective and subjective data are listed in Table 2.

Table 2. Objective and Subjective Data Issues.

Objective	Subjective
• Financial expenses, donations, and consumption • Observable behaviour, e.g., prosocial actions and delinquency • How time is spent, e.g., working 14 hours a day • Big data/Spatial data, e.g., human mobility, transactions, and online login	• Personal, user experience • Questions using likert scale "agree/disagree" • Focus group discussions

Malay restricted blocks, i.e., too many Malay households

Chinese restricted blocks, i.e., too many Chinese households

Indian restricted blocks, i.e., too many Indian households

Fig. 1. Spatial Ethnic Representation.
Source: Leong *et al.* (2020).

In the following section, we will display examples of the different data types. Figure 1 is an example of *spatial data*, an objective measure of residential neighbourhoods that reveal ethnic concentration, i.e., residents are clustered according to their racial background (Leong *et al.*, 2020).

When looking at the following data, one might ask the following question: What is the policy implication of this data? What does it mean

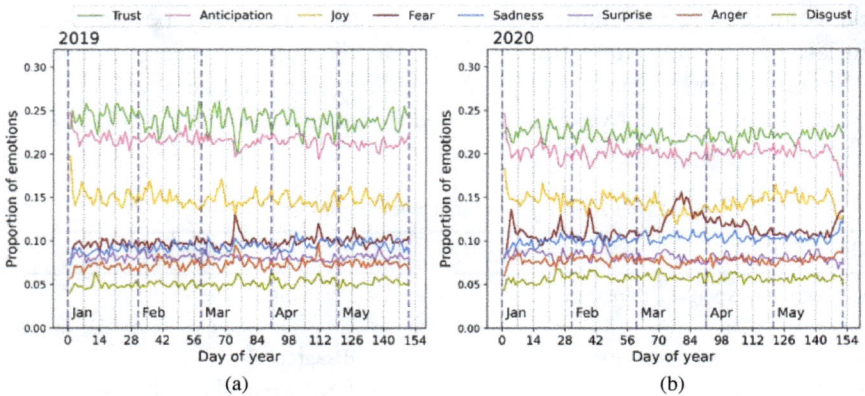

Fig. 2.　Emotion Proportion by Types During COVID-19 of (a) 2019 and (b) 2020.

for ethnic-based service delivery? Further points of analysis may include the following: Does residential proximity to places of worship, or social service centers have any potential correlations to residents' physical or mental health, or to levels of social trust amongst members of the community? Is there the presence of amenities that may aid in alleviating social vulnerability amongst socially disadvantaged residents and clients?

Next, we move on to the next example, which is of Big Data. In this study by Yan *et al.* (2021), data was collected on the emotions expressed in Tweets during the COVID-19 'lockdown' (i.e., Circuit Breaker) in Singapore and used to give a birds-eye view of the sentiments among different subgroups in the local populace. As observed in Fig. 2, when comparing 2019 and 2020, significantly more 'fear'-related tweets were posted during the COVID-19 'lockdown' in Singapore in 2020 (Yan *et al.*, 2021), as indicated by the spike in the red line of the graph on the right, as indicated by the blue arrow.

In Table 3 and Fig. 3, tweets were then sorted according to the language they were posted in, and sentiment analysis was once conducted. From this data, researchers were able to identify differences in the sentiments of individuals of different subgroups in Singapore, with certain communities being more affected by the lockdown than others. Using Twitter's data, we could see that there are significant variations in the pandemic experiences among different subgroups in Singapore, such as

Table 3. The Top 10 Languages Used in COVID-19 Related Tweets in Singapore.

Rank	Language	Number of Tweets	Percentage (%)
1	English	5,433,782	84.51
2	Malay	259,485	4.04
3	Japanese	170,802	2.66
4	Indonesian	151,604	2.36
5	Korean	84,960	1.32
6	Filipino	61,019	0.95
7	Chinese	48,855	0.76
8	Tamil	40,946	0.64
9	Thai	30,894	0.48
10	Hindi	18,578	0.29
	Other languages	128,524	1.99
	Total	6,429,449	100.00

the Japanese subgroup, which had significantly higher levels of sentiments of 'anticipation,' as compared to other subgroups in Singapore. This data may serve to inform policy and program decisions, allowing the evidence-based allocation of resources to subgroups which may need it the most.

A surprising finding arose when COVID-19-related tweets originating from Singapore were ranked from highest to lowest in quantity, according to the language in which they were published. Following English, in which 84.51% of quotes were published, the three next top languages with the highest number of tweets were Malay (4.04%), Japanese (2.66%), and Indonesian (2.36%), all of which were groups which constituted a relatively smaller percentage of the local populace (i.e., minority groups) (Yan *et al.*, 2021). This analysis also reflected the kind of communication platforms on which members of different communities may engage in conversations and discuss current issues.

To round up this sub-chapter, let us recall our example of the Child Aid program that was mentioned in the previous chapter (Fig. 4 and Table 4). In this example, what individual-level or group-level data can one collect? Based on the context of the community that this organization serves, what would be the data that would be the most relevant to collect?

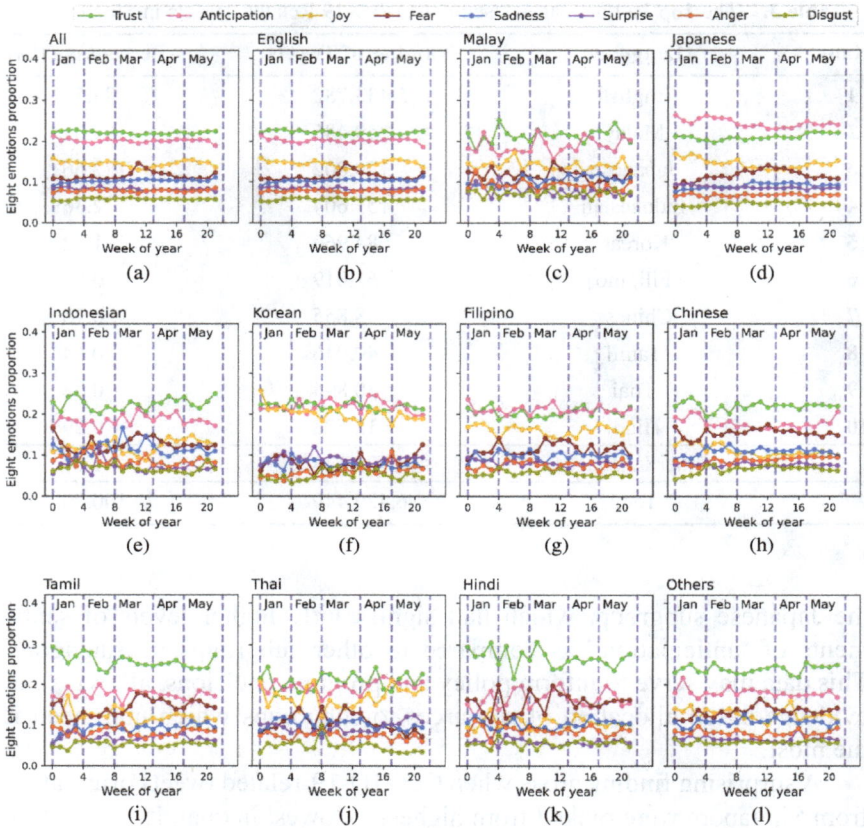

Fig. 3.   Behavioral Responses by Nationalities.
Source: Yan *et al.* (2021).

Fig. 4.   Children's Reaction and Slum Dwellings.

Table 4. Hypothetical Example — Child Aid.

Clarity of Purpose	Child Aid — provide food, uniform, and other allowance for children from low-income families to stay afloat
Scope	Promote education and uplift welfare of children from poverty households
Stakeholder Engagement	Collaborate with schools, VWOs, and family counsellors
Materiality	Monetary cost of provision, manpower, etc.
Comparative	School dropout rate, percentage child labour in province, duration of program, location of schools, percentage completed primary education
Transparency	Getting credible data from Govt, NGOs
Verification	Independent audit
Embeddedness	Annual budget, buy-in from local authorities, NGOs

Table 5 lists a few examples of individual-level and group-level data that can be collected for this hypothetical example. Can you think of any other types of individual-level and group-level data that can be collected?

Table 5. Examples of Individual and Group Data.

Examples of Individual-Level Data	Examples of Group-Level Data
• In-depth child interview	• Dropout rate of schools
• In-depth parent interview	• Socio-economic status of schools
• Amount of money received by child	• Percentage child-labour in province
• School attendance of child	• Percentage completed primary education
• Academic grade of child	
• Number of friends child has	
• Health status of child	
• Feedback from social workers	

Data Measurement

In this section, we discuss data measurement, how data should be managed, and its impact to the social impact evaluation. It is crucial that data is measured and captured accurately so that it is able to accurately reflect the social impact that needs to be examined. There are four key areas to note when it comes to data measurement.

Cross-Sectional Study	Longitudinal Study
Comparing different groups at the same time	Analyze same group over time

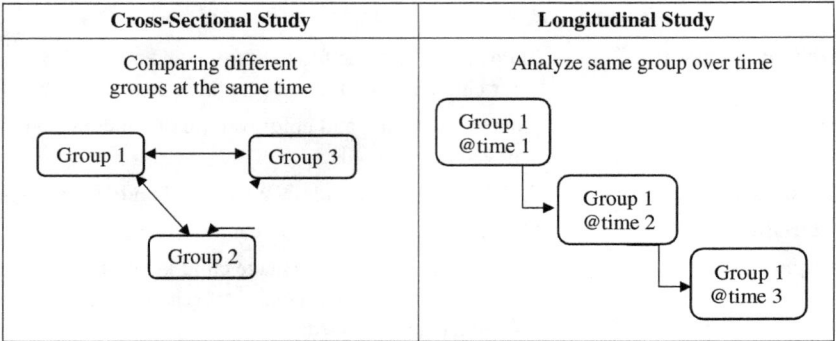

Fig. 5.   Types of Study.

(i) Cause and effect

Can the outcome be attributed to the social service agency's program or intervention, or has it come about due to natural changes that occur over time? For instance, a country may report a reduction in the sentiments of fear or anxiety related to COVID-19 — this might not be attributed to the implemented lockdown measures but instead to the overall populace growing more accustomed to a pandemic life as it wears on.

Generally, there are two research designs in empirical research — cross-sectional studies and longitudinal studies (Fig. 5). Cross-sectional studies take place at one specific point in time, during which they enable the comparison of different groups at the same time. On the other hand, longitudinal studies extend beyond one particular point in time and allow the same group to be compared over time (Thomas, 2020). Hence, despite longitudinal studies being more costly and coming with their fair share of challenges (e.g., manage dropouts of study participants by attempting to keep them interested and engaged throughout the study duration — possibly by offering remuneration to them for their time), they are deemed to be more robust than cross-sectional studies. As longitudinal studies enable the researcher to draw conclusions about cause-and-effect, they are hence generally deemed to be more preferable than cross-sectional studies.

(ii) Reliability

Another important point of consideration is the concept of reliability or precision, i.e., does the measurement provide us a consistent reading? One example would be the contactless forehead scan thermometers that are often used at the entrances of buildings (e.g., shopping malls and educational institutions) during the COVID-19 pandemic in Singapore. One might wonder, are the readings taken reliable? If a person's measured temperature fluctuates widely every time it is taken by the thermometer, this would suggest that the equipment is not reliable. Recalling the example of the Child Aid program that has been cited in the current and previous chapters. In this case, unreliability may be attributed to human factors: if there is a high turnover rate of teachers at a particular school, the record of a child's attendance in class may not be reliable as different teachers may embrace different standards in recording class attendance. It may also be noted that the concept of 'reliability' in social sciences might be similar to that of 'precision' in the 'hard' social sciences.

(iii) Validity
The third notable point is the concept of validity, i.e., are you measuring what you intend to measure? While reliability seeks to understand the consistency of reading, validity aims to find out if the reading is an appropriate representation of the measure we intend to assess. Using the previous example of a scan thermometer, a question of validity may be as follows: Does the temperature taken on the forehead using a scan thermometer provide a good indication of fever or body temperature? The instrument may produce a reliable (i.e., consistent) reading of temperature on the forehead, but is it a valid measure of a fever? In general, there are a few types of validity, which are listed in order from least to most robust:

1. *Face validity*
   • Face validity offers some form of superficial affirmation that the instrument measures what it intends to measure. For instance, to find out if an individual is trustworthy, we could ask the person if they have ever "cheated in an examination," or "knowingly short change another person." This will have at least some aspects of face validity, though one may argue that an untrustworthy person will not be forthcoming about their past misbehaviours.
2. *Conceptual validity*
   • Conceptual validity offers more concrete, robust insights into the underlying measurement or latent dimensions that we want to capture. For example, monetary incentives offered to children from vulnerable families to remain in school provide an assessment of direct educational support. Questions can also be posed questions indirectly with the aim of reducing desirability bias, for instance, instead of asking if an individual considers himself or herself as

extrovert, we asked questions on how much they enjoy travelling, meeting new people, or engaging in outdoor activities.

3. *Convergence validity*
   - Measurement validity can also be discussed in the form of convergence validity. In a nutshell, does the measurement converge with other instruments for similar constructs? We should expect a significant correlation if the measurements are tapping on the same dimension. The measurement of extroversion, for instance, would expectedly echo findings from similar instruments that assessment a person's proclivity to outdoor activities, social engagement, or appetite for adventures.

4. *Predictive validity*
   - Predictive validity is the pinnacle of all validation. In the broadest sense, we like to know if this instrument can predict the actual outcome as postulated in a longitudinal design. For instance, children from vulnerable families who stay in schools will receive more education and, thus, empower them with better employment opportunities. As such, predictive validation is established when the child's past attendance in school predicts their future quality of life.

Reliability and validity are two important methodological and analytical concepts in social sciences. Just like the similarity between reliability and precision, 'validity' in the social sciences is also akin to 'accuracy' in the 'hard' social sciences. In other words, "precision–accuracy" is used in 'hard' social sciences such as statistics and geography, while psychology (and possibly when examining social policies in social work and/or sociology), on the other hand, speaks of "reliability–validity," as it measures latent constructs.

To give a more concrete example of reliability–validity, supposing we want to develop a measure of "quality of life," what data should we consider? In this case, there are several types of data (individual-level and group-level data) and measurement issues (reliability and validity, objective vs. subjective, sample vs. population) — the former includes questions on personal income, education, health status, and other subjective ratings on well-being; the latter includes indicators on national income, literacy, crime rate, and national opinion polls (Table 6).

Table 6. Levels of Quality of Life Measure.

Individual Level	Group Level
• Personal income	• National income
• Education	• Employment rate
• Health status	• Home ownership
• Marital status	• Education/Literacy rate
• No. of children	• Life expectancy
• Civic participation	• Crime rate
• Attendance in programs	• Philanthropic donations
• Family relations	• Opinion polls, surveys
• Life satisfaction	
• Socio-economic security	

Hence, as we attempt to answer the empirical question, it is essential to ensure that the research data obtained is reliable and valid, and ascertain whether objective, subjective, or both types of data are being utilized. Measurable, objective data is favoured over subjective evaluation for greater reliability.

(iv) Sampling and participant recruitment
As it is very costly and challenging to collect data from all members of a population, random samples that are representative of the research population are more often utilized in data collection. However, collecting data from a random sample of individuals in a targeted population is often contaminated with some form of bias they are often harder to contact. Individuals from vulnerable families, for instance, may be reluctant to share with the investigators out of concern for privacy and for fear of retribution.

For some research, a convenience sampling approach is adopted due to limitations in resources or other constraints — a convenient sample is collected using the most accessible method. It is a form of non-random sampling method, and the external validity of the study would be limited, as the characteristics, experience, and sentiments of the non-random sample might not be representative of the general populace, or target group the study hopes to reach out to. For instance, in public opinion studies conducted prior to the 2020 U.S. general elections, Joe Biden was in the lead by about 5–10% points. However, when it came to the actual results of polling day, it was revealed that only 2% more Americans had voted for Joe Biden than Donald Trump. This shows that the pre-voting public opinion survey had garnered responses from a convenience sample of the population, which was not representative of all Americans. It might be inferred that Donald Trump's supporters might have abstained from taking the pre-voting survey, in fear of being stigmatized or critiqued for their political opinions.

In order to ensure sample biases is minimized, we typically aim to collect a larger sample, and from a wide range of sources as much as possible. In general, the size of the random error variance will decrease as sample size increases; moreover, a large sample offers researchers the option to weight-specific cases that are under-represented. The investigators can assign greater importance to certain characteristics that are disproportionately less than what it should be, i.e., fewer respondents with these characteristics took part in the research.

Supporting Data from Multiple Studies and Levels

We have discussed the different types of data, such as objective-subjective measurements, individual- and group-level data, and analytical considerations such as sampling, and reliability–validity. Hence, a question that one may ask is as follows: Why do we need to measure different levels of data?

Social science research that is both robust and insightful tend to be measurable and replicable. As a matter of fact, it is useful to measure different levels of data as confidence in research is enhanced when different databases, and different levels of analysis produce the same conclusion. In addition, multi-level and multi-site studies enable us to examine possible interaction effects between individual-level and group-level data — which means that individuals from different backgrounds react differently depending on the external environment. In this case, interaction is said to exist, and this signifies that a one-size-fits-all policy may not work well.

Such interaction effects are exemplified in a study by Roy *et al.* (2016), which examines the impact of neighbourhood-relative income and subjective social status on one's physical and mental health. Both individual-level and group-level data on income were obtained, which helped identified the interaction effect between the two (Fig. 6).

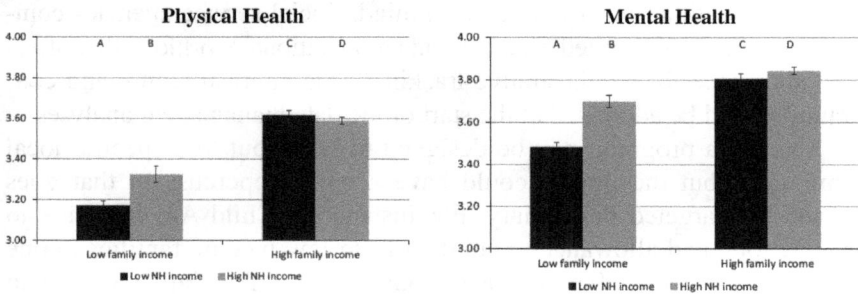

Fig. 6. Public and Mental Health of Income Groups.
Source: Roy *et al.* (2016).

From the diagram above, we can observe that lower-income families generally reported lower physical and mental health compared to higher-income families, i.e., the twin bars on the left of each diagram are consistently lower compared to the twin bars on the right of each diagram. A closer examination, however, suggests that lower-income families demonstrate better physical and mental health when they live in higher-income neighbourhoods. In other words, it is better to be a poor man in a rich neighbourhood, than a poor man in a poor neighbourhood) (Roy *et al.*, 2016).

Hence, in this example, family/household income (individual-level data) interacted with neighbourhood income (group-level data) to influence one's physical and mental health (outcomes), and similar trends were observed in Singapore (e.g., Leong *et al.*, 2021b). Interventions can be targeted in vulnerable neighbourhoods to serve needy families.

Some Key Attention by Agency on Data Management

Taking an overarching view, what are the key takeaways for social service agencies on data management? First, program evaluation is an integral aspect of social service delivery to ensure sound corporate governance, strategic planning, and accountability. By extension, data management — which is the pillar for impact evaluation and assessment — is a part of the larger analytical framework. Relevant data should be meticulously collected and maintained with a longer-term goal in mind. Social service agencies commonly operate with limited finances and an operational workload that offers little allowance for administrative tracking. This political reality and constraints should be addressed at the start of the data management analyses.

Second, a program may be designed to reach out to a specific local community, but the impact could have a wider repercussion that goes beyond the targeted beneficiary. For instance, a Child Aid initiative to provide food and allowance to children from low-income families in one school could have galvanized a regional support for similar causes in other neighbourhoods. The broader impact should therefore be assessed at the provincial level. In this case, a more comprehensive impact evaluation would require data at the regional level, information that may be otherwise not accessible to the social service agencies.

Lastly, robust data management and analysis and appreciation for social impact evaluation would require multidisciplinary knowledge of statistics, research methods, corporate governance, and public policies. Practitioners in social service agencies will need the support and encouragement from academia, social service regulatory authorities, and civil societies to ensure that the evaluations and analyses are performed to most rigorous standards.

Conclusion

This chapter offered an overview of data management and analyses for social impact analysis. We introduced the different genres of databases (e.g., individual- vs. group-level data, objective vs. subjective data, and sample vs. population data) and other conceptual and measurement-related considerations, such as reliability, validity, and research designs (e.g., cross-sectional vs. longitudinal). In the increasing complex and interwoven climate, the social service sector will need to fall back on evidence-based empirical research to fine-tune its professional development and service delivery. The type of data, methodology, and analytical approach are the tools to achieve this purpose and to ensure there is robust policy formulation and deliberation. This chapter does not cover the full range of methodological and data analytics, but instead, it is written with the aim of inspiring social service practitioners to be cognizant of their own environment and the potential to continually enhance their programs and services through social impact evaluation.

Bibliography

Leong, C.H., Chin, W.C.B., Feng, C.-C., and Wang, Y.-C. (2021a). A socio-ecological perspective on COVID-19 spatiotemporal integrated vulnerability in Singapore. In Shaw, S.L. and Sui, D. (Ed.), *Mapping COVID-19 in Space and Time: Understanding the Spatial and Temporal Dynamics of a Global Pandemic*, pp. 81–111. Springer, Cham. https://doi.org/10.1007/978-3-030-72808-3_6.

Leong, C.H., Tan, S.J., Minton, E.A., and Tambyah, S.K. (2021b). Economic hardship and neighborhood diversity: Influences on consumer well-being. *Journal of Consumer Affairs*. https://doi.org/10.1111/joca.12365.

Leong, C.H., Teng, E., and Ko, W. (2020). The state of ethnic congregation in Singapore today. In Leong C.H. and Malone-Lee L.C. (Ed.), *Building Resilient Neighborhoods: The Convergence of Policies, Research, and Practice*, pp. 29–49, Singapore: Springer. https://doi.org/10.1007/978-981-13-7048-9_3.

Leong, C.H. and Yap, Y. (2020). Geographic segregation in Singapore: The emerging schism in our social contour. In Chong, T. (Ed), *Navigating Differences: Integration in Singapore*, pp. 231–247. Singapore: ISEAS.

Roy, A.L., Godfrey, E.B., and Rarick, J.R.D. (2016). Do we know where we stand? Neighborhood relative income, subjective social status, and health. *American Journal of Community Psychology*, 57, 448–458.

Yan, Y., Chin, W.C.B., Leong, C.H., Wang, Y.-C., and Feng, C.-C. (2021). Emotional responses through COVID-19 in Singapore. In Shaw, S.L. and Sui, D. (Ed.), *Mapping COVID-19 in Space and Time: Understanding the Spatial and Temporal Dynamics of a Global Pandemic*, pp. 61–79. Springer. https://doi.org/10.1007/978-3-030-72808-3_5.

https://doi.org/10.1142/9789819815036_0003

Chapter 3

Measuring the Social Impact of Programmes[*]

Leong Chan-Hoong[†] and Angelica Ang Ting Yi[††]

[†]*S. Rajaratnam School of International Studies (RSIS), Nanyang Technological University, Singapore*

[††]*National University of Singapore, Singapore*

Abstract

Social impact may be defined as the positive change that an organization has created over time. This change could have the same effect as the work of an organization on people and their communities, and it could be motivated by activities, programmes, or policies put in place. In this chapter, we will discuss the social outcomes of programmes and projects and the importance of measuring the social impact. We will touch upon the use of indicators in measuring social outcomes and their limitations. The type of measurements commonly applied for measuring outcomes will also be discussed along with the implications of social impact findings for service delivery. We will use various programmes, case studies, and social policies to illustrate how the different social evaluation frameworks can be applied for impact analyses.

---

[*]This chapter was originally published in C. H. Leong and A. T. Y. Ang (2021). *Social Service Leadership Exchange Programme Lecture Series*. NUS Department of Social Work.

Introduction

Social impacts are the changes that organizations make as a result of their interventions, programmes, or policies. Measuring social impact needs huge amounts of resources and expertise, and might even require external help from stakeholders, some of whom may not be forthcoming with the rendering of assistance (Future Learn, n.d.; Zappalà and Lyons, 2009).

Since there might be limited time and resource constraints, should one still measure social impact? In fact, there is a trade-off to social impact measurement. In some situations, measuring social impact can be a distraction and a drain on limited resources. For instance, in the aftermath of a natural disaster, the imminent need is to feed and provide shelter for the masses. During such humanitarian emergencies, many organizations engage in relief efforts, and hence it might become exceedingly difficult to measure the influence of a single organization in the whole relief programme (Hanna, 2010).

However, this is not to say that any attempt at social impact measurement is unnecessary. In fact, there are several key reasons why it is important for organizations to measure the social impact of their work (Miesing, n.d.). Firstly, social impact measurement might be beneficial for (i) funders and stakeholders. It allows one to tell a meaningful story about the change they have made, which can be useful material for recruiting new funders. Funding agencies and stakeholders may also wish to know how their money was spent, and what has been achieved with the money contributed to a programme or organization. Social impact measurement is also beneficial to (ii) the organization, aiding in the assessment of which programmes are working and which are not, thereby allowing the organization to shift its limited resources accordingly. This measurement can also highlight if an organization is on track to achieving its long-term mission and vision. That said, one might run into some challenges when measuring social impact. The following are several key questions that may be asked by organizations embarking on social impact measurement, followed by a discussion on the theories, ideas, and frameworks pertinent to the questions:

- What does it really mean to "do good"?
- How can we relate "doing good" with financial values?
- How can we identify the cause and effect of the social programmes?
- How can we collect data that are usable for analysis?
- How can we make sure that we are interpreting the data correctly?

Method 1. Social Accounting and Audit

There are three methods to measuring social impact. The first is Social Accounting and Audit (SAA), which we will unpack further in this section. SAA is the "systematic analysis of the effects of an organisation on its communities of interest or stakeholders, with stakeholder input as part of the data that are analysed for the accounting statement" (Future Learn, n.d.). This method is akin to how financial audits are used to provide financial information relevant to shareholders, and SAA is used to provide information relevant to society (Gibbon and Dey, 2011).

Why should SAA be adopted by an organization to measure social impact? There are two main benefits of SAA. Firstly, there is no need for new information, as the SAA model largely relies on existing information which organizations already possess. Secondly, there is no need for external auditors when utilizing the SAA model, which can be thought of as an internal audit — organizations identify their own values and objectives, and then report on how well they are achieving them (Zappalà and Lyons, 2009).

There are eight principles of SAA, which have been further elaborated upon in Table 1.

Table 1. The Social Accounting and Audit (SAA) Model.

No.	Principle of SAA	Guiding Question	Hypothetical Example: Child Aid
1	Clarity of Purpose	Why are we doing this?	Provide food, uniforms, and other allowances for children from low-income families to stay inschool
2	Scope	What are our values, objectives, and stakeholders?	Promote education and uplift the welfare of children from poverty-stricken households
3	Stakeholder Engagement	Are we engaging with a wide variety of stakeholders who are related to our organization?	Collaborate with schools, VWOs, and family counsellors
4	Materiality	What needs to be included in the social accounts?	Monetary cost of provision, manpower, etc.

(Continued)

Table 1.   (*Continued*)

No.	Principle of SAA	Guiding Question	Hypothetical Example: Child Aid
5	Comparative	Are we using appropriate benchmarks, targets, and external standards for our performance comparisons?	The school dropout rate, % of child labour in the province, duration of the programme, location of schools, % completed primary education
6	Transparency	Have we demonstrated that our findings are accurate and honest?	Getting credible data from the government, NGOs
7	Verification	Has an independent social audit panel verified the social accounts?	Independent audit
8	Embeddedness	Is the SAA process embedded in our organization's life cycle and practices?	Annual budget, buy-in from local authorities, NGOs

Source: Zappalà and Lyons (2009, p. 10).

Next, this section will explore the steps taken to conduct SAA. There are three main steps involved, which are as follows (Zappalà and Lyons, 2009):

1. Planning
   - Identify the organization's mission, objectives, and values.
   - This step is important, as it reveals the "essence" of an organization. In other words, this step explains what an organization does, why it exists, and who it works with (and for).
2. Accounting
   - Identify the scope of the social accounting process.
   - Set up relevant information-gathering systems in order to enable the organization to report on its performance (against its mission, objectives, and values).
   - Compile and analyze the information collected.
3. Reporting and Audit
   - Information collected must be interpreted and audited by a panel of impartial individuals. This ensures that the report is correctly prepared and can be considered to be a fair and honest reflection of the events that have occurred. If the panel is satisfied, the final report is made publicly available to funders and stakeholders.

- The organization may use the findings to (i) review if its objectives are still appropriate for the present day, (ii) set new targets for the following year, (iii) identify if the stakeholders are benefitting from the organization's programmes, and (iv) justify the organization's existence.

Now, the above-mentioned three steps of SAA (Table 2) will be illustrated through a case study to analyze how SAA can be performed for the

Table 2. Steps of SAA Process.

No.	Steps of SAA Process	Case Study: All Saints Action Network (ASAN)
1	Planning	Mission: To "work in partnership to create a sustainable organisation responsive to local needs through the development and management of enterprise, employment, and environmental projects."
		Objectives: ASAN is a social enterprise, and its objectives are to improve the quality of life for those who live and work in All Saints through the creation of jobs (e.g., nursery), and provision of local services (e.g., recycling services) and training opportunities (e.g., social value consultancy).
2	Accounting	ASAN wants to determine what impact it is making on the community of All Saints.
		To do this, ASAN regularly engages its stakeholders to gather feedback about the outcomes and the services it provides for the community.
		The data collected include performance indicators and the types of consultation and engagement with stakeholders.
		In this social accounting period, ASAN has an income of £788,548, and it has expended a total of £785,554; 70% of the income was generated through enterprise activity, which is an improvement on the 61% over the last social accounting period; 10% of the money ASAN spends goes to local businesses within the WV2 area of Wolverhampton and a further 21% is spent on Wolverhampton-based businesses.
3	Reporting and Audit	SAA is performed on an annual basis in ASAN. The organization shared the findings with its stakeholders regularly as a means to engage and improve relations between the two.

Source: Karim and Baker (2014).

All Saints Action Network (ASAN), a community enterprise located in All Saints, Wolverhampton.

Despite the various benefits of SAA, this method of social impact measurement also comes with its own set of limitations. Much time is required for measuring social accounts and drafting social reports. Staff and volunteers from social services organizations need to keep track of the areas of the project where the financial contributions were made (i.e., input), a task that is both arduous and time-consuming. Keeping track of and quantifying the monetary and non-monetary resources devoted to different areas of work (e.g., direct counselling, stakeholder engagement, administrative matters, and training) is also a complex task, making SAA an expensive endeavour (Zappalà and Lyons, 2009).

Method 2: Logic Models

The next social impact measurement model is the logic model. Logic models are hypothesized descriptions of a series of gradual, sequential steps that establish cause and effect (Julien, 1997). If X, Y, and Z are events,

- If X happens, then Y will happen.
- If Y happens, then Z will happen.
- If Z happens, the programme goals will be achieved.

Instead of focusing on outputs, logic models focus on the outcomes of a programme. In other words, if certain activities (i.e., X) take place, certain outputs (i.e., Y) should occur, and certain outcomes (i.e., Z) should consequently arise. In essence, this is a framework that enables organizations to incorporate evaluations into a programme's design phase. This is important as most evaluations are conducted at the end of a programme — and this can be problematic because a large-scale programme can go off-course halfway. There are a few distinct benefits in the logic model approach (Zappalà and Lyons, 2009).

Firstly, this method enables the staff to appreciate the fact that the programme is nested within the broader organizational mission and context. It encourages the staff to see how different and seemingly disparaged activities in a programme are linked to each other in a meaningful way. Secondly, it facilitates the clear identification of a programme's objectives and results, and it provides a structured starting point for identifying activities, implementation details, costs, and monitoring criteria. Thirdly, the findings serve as a summary of the project, as an important means to update and engage funders and stakeholders. Lastly, it facilitates social impact evaluation as all members in the organization can connect with this process; it simplifies internal evaluations, repositioning it as a learning process rather than an appraisal in time.

One application for the logic model is programme planning, starting with the end goal in mind and working back. In using the logic model for evaluation, six questions must be addressed in chronological order as mentioned in Table 3 (Julien, 1997). In the next segment, we will use the Ethnic Integration Policy (EIP) in Singapore to illustrate how the series of questions can help develop a logic model for social impact evaluation.

The EIP is a race-based residential quota system to prevent the formation of racial enclaves in Singapore (Wee, 1989). This policy was implemented in 1989, and was designed to address a growing housing segregation along racial lines where prospective home buyers relocate to neighbourhoods according to their ethnic profile. In the long run, racially clustered neighbourhoods will reduce opportunities for social mixing and

Table 3. Logic Model Questions.

No.	Question of Logic Model	Case Study: Ethnic Integration Policy (EIP) in Singapore in 1989
1	What is the current situation?	Singaporeans want to live alongside people of the same ethnicity, i.e., racial segregation.
2	What does the ideal situation look like?	Singaporeans of all ethnicities live, work, and play alongside each other.
3	What behaviours must be modified in order for us to achieve the ideal situation?	Choice of housing location, not rejecting neighbours of another race.
4	What knowledge/skills must individuals acquire in order to modify their behaviours?	Appreciation of how EIP works and the reason for the implementation.
5	What activities must be conducted in order for the required knowledge/skills to be acquired?	Housing quota imposed on apartment blocks based on the racial identity of the household (i.e., Chinese, Malay, Indian).
6	What resources are needed for these activities?	The government is able to influence the housing market and home ownership. Close to 80% of Singaporeans live in public housing, and the state is able to influence home pricing, availability, and mortgage payment.

Source: Leong *et al.* (2020).

hamper the nation's progress to building a multi-racial society. This policy imposes a standard quota for each racial group in every public housing apartment block and at the neighbourhood level. The quotas, the comparison against the population distribution of each racial group, and the percentage residing in HDB flats are reported in Table 4.

Based on the logic model, we can break down the thought process behind the design of the EIP. As the EIP ensures that people of diverse racial and religious backgrounds live together as neighbours (X), it may be assumed that the close proximity between them would facilitate contact (Y), and hence foster acceptance and/or tolerance between them (Z). Despite the government's valiant efforts, a preference for racial segregation remains a housing policy challenge even after 30 years. A study conducted by Leong *et al.* (2020) found that the percentage of blocks that have met any ethnic quota over the years has increased from 24.4% in 1989 to 34.0% over the last 30 years, and it will likely continue to rise in spite of the implementation of the EIP (Tables 5 and 6).

As shown in Fig. 1, EIP data are visualized and projected on a map of Singapore. It depicts distinct spatial patterns of the places of residence among different racial groups in Singapore, with the ethnic Chinese generally concentrated around the central area, while ethnic minorities (i.e., Malays and Indians) are scattered around the fringes of the island state.

In evaluating the outcome of EIP, it is clear there remains some form of ethnic segregation and thus there is room for improvement. Let us explore how the EIP may be further improved using questions 3–6 of the logic model as a framework for our analysis (see Table 7).

Should your organization select this method for social impact measurement, which logic model would you pick? There are many variants of

Table 4.   Ethnic Quotas, Population Distribution and Residence.

Races	Block Limit (%)	Neighbourhood Limit (%)	Population Distribution (%)	Reside in HDB Dwelling (%)
Chinese	87	84	74	81.3
Malays	25	22	14	96.8
Indians/others	15	12	12	82.7

Source: Leong *et al.* (2020).

Table 5.   Percentage of Blocks Meeting Ethnic Quota.

1989	2016	2017	2018	2019	2020
24.2	27.9	29.6	30.0	33.7	34.0

Table 6. Percentage of Blocks that have Met Each Type of Ethnic Quota.

	Chinese	Malay	Indian	At least one
2016	17.7	4.7	6.8	27.9
2017	18.4	4.6	8.5	29.6
2018	19.5	4.8	7.7	30.0
2019	18.0	8.9	9.1	33.7
2020	17.2	10.6	9.3	34.0

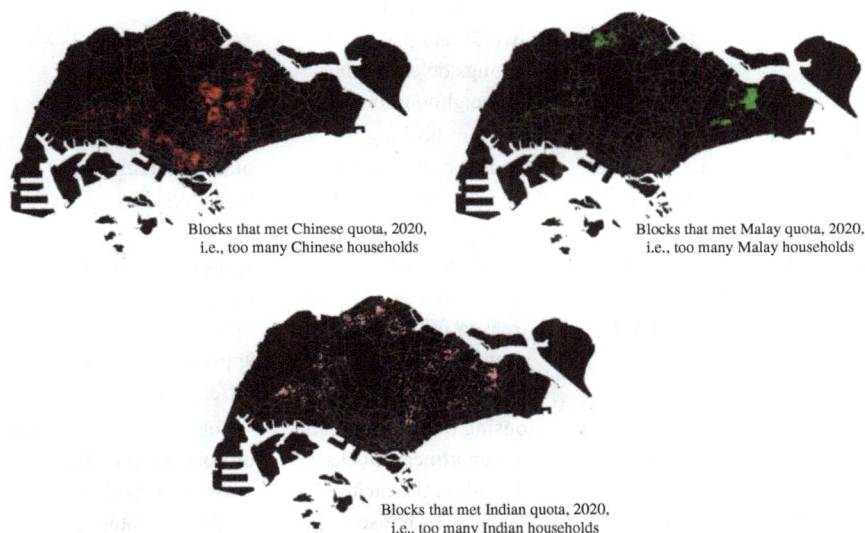

Blocks that met Chinese quota, 2020, i.e., too many Chinese households

Blocks that met Malay quota, 2020, i.e., too many Malay households

Blocks that met Indian quota, 2020, i.e., too many Indian households

Fig. 1. Locations of HDB Blocks that Have Met the Three Ethnic Quotas.

Source: Leong *et al.* (2020).

the logic model, and while some are proprietary, the most common model framework is the Logical Framework Analysis or LogFrame (Zappalà and Lyons, 2009). Logframe is a mandatory framework for social service agencies applying for government funding in countries like Australia, Canada, and New Zealand. There are several key characteristics of LogFrame. It is a systematic way of identifying the elements in a pro-gramme and the linkages between them, and it is applicable to all stages of a programme, like a living document. When executed correctly, it serves to clearly articulate and document a programme's theory of change (Zappalà and Lyons, 2009).

Figure 2 is a guide to LogFrame, adopted from Nichols (1999).

Table 7.   Case Study: Ethnic Integration Policy in Singapore.

No.	Question of Logic Model	Current Status in 2020	What Improvement is Needed?
1	What is the current situation?	Singaporeans still prefer living alongside people of the same ethnicity, i.e., racial segregation.	Desegregation, and encourage home buyers to look beyond the racial or economic background of the neighbourhood.
2	What does the ideal situation look like?	Singaporeans of all ethnicities to live, work, and play alongside each other in neighbourhoods.	–
3	What behaviours must be modified in order for us to achieve the ideal situation?	Choice of housing location, do not reject neighbours of another race.	Negative stereotypes of other ethnicities need to be addressed.
4	What knowledge/skills must individuals acquire in order to modify their behaviours?	Appreciation of how EIP works and the reason for the implementation.	Singaporeans must be willing to learn about other cultures in order to appreciate cultural differences.
5	What activities must be conducted in order for the required knowledge/skills to be acquired?	Housing quotas imposed on apartment blocks based on the racial identity of households (i.e., Chinese, Malay, Indian).	More outreach efforts must be conducted at the grassroots level in order to increase inter-ethnic interactions.
6	What resources are needed for these activities?	The government is able to influence the housing market and home ownership. Close to 80% of Singaporeans live in public housing, and the state is able to influence home pricing, availability, and mortgage payment.	More budget and volunteers.

LOGFRAME GUIDE

The logframe is a **SUMMARY** of the project, to answer the questions
WHY the project is being done, and **WHAT IMPACT** the project will have.

	Hierarchy of Objectives	Verifiable Indicators	Means of Verification	Assumptions
this will contribute to the goal	**Goal** 1. Broad. Project contributes to the overall goal	Usually not necessary as too general and hard to measure in limited time period	What records will be kept What methods of data and information gathering will be used?	What must hold true for the rationale to work What risks exist to not achieving ultimate goal
we anticipate the purpose will result. If the purpose is achieved, then	**Purpose** 1. (2 if necessary) The use/result/immediate impact of the project Include beneficiaries in statement	Explains the extent of the results at end-of-project. QQT-quality, quantity, time Used for evaluating the project	eg. baselines surveys, government records minutes of meetings trip reports training evaluations	What must hold true for the purpose to result from the outputs.
we produce the outputs. If we produce the outputs then	**Outputs** 1-4 What we produce. What the management is responsible for achieving.	Express the scope of the project. How many? What type? Use for monitoring the project	as above	What conditions must remain valid for the activities to result in the outputs.
If we do the activities, then	**Activities** 1-4 for each output What we actually do	**Summary of Inputs** Mention total budget and inputs of various participants		**Conditions Precedent** Agreements or inputs necessary to begin project Policy or activity of other agencies required

The question of **HOW** the project should be implemented should be addressed in the
NARRATIVE, ACTIVITY SCHEDULE and **BUDGET** of the proposal.

Source: IDSS, An Introduction to the Logframe Approach, 1999.

Fig. 2. Log-frame Guides.

Source: Nichols (1999).

Beyond the key benefits in aiding social impact measurement, what are the limitations of logic models? There are several. Firstly, the causal logic used to underpin a programme can only be as good as the quality of evidence that exists to support a particular intervention. Secondly, logic models are theoretical frameworks, and reality does not always follow the projected paths. In other words, as logic models are based on an "if this, then that" mode of thinking, the reality on the ground tends to be more complex, dynamic, and networked. In addition, variables outside the model could influence programme outcomes. Hence, programmes may at times have unintended consequences that are unaccounted for in the model.

Let us examine a real-world example of an organization's programme, whereby unintended consequences had arisen. In accordance with the logic model, the programme aimed to distribute mosquito nets to individuals living in malaria-prone areas (X), with the assumption that individuals would use the nets to protect themselves from mosquitoes (Y), consequently resulting in a decrease in the incidence rate of malaria (Z). However, when implemented on the ground, the mosquito nets that were given out were used to protect crops and as fishing nets, chicken coops, and even wedding veils (Bush and Short, 2016; Carrington, 2018; Owens, 2019)! Hence, we can never always be certain that X leads to Y, and Y to Z, which is a crucial point to think about when deciding on the tool of choice for social impact measurement.

Method 3: Social Return on Investment

Finally, the third method is Social Return on Investment, or SROI. SROI measures the value generated by a programme. This encompasses more than the dollars and cents that one may see in the organization's balance sheet, as it may include the social, environmental, and economic value (Future Learn, n.d.). Despite being rather similar to SAA, SROI has one incredibly unique, salient, feature — the opportunity costs, a factor which is not considered in SAA or logic models. SROI also requires a lot of estimation, which might result in potential differences between organizations, due to the subjectivity of the judgement of the evaluator(s). Broadly speaking, there are two main categories of SROIs: Evaluative SROIs and Forecast SROIs. The former are conducted retrospectively and are based on outcomes that have already taken place. The latter are used to predict how much social value will be created if activities meet their desired outcomes.

There are many benefits to using the SROI approach. Like other social impact evaluation methods, it helps improve performance measurement, programme planning, and evaluation. Incorporating opportunity cost accounting enables organizations to better demonstrate the actual social impact of targeted programmes, facilitates the comparison of impact across organizations, and raises the profile of the organization through both internal and external stakeholder engagement. The SROI formula is based on the assessed monetary values of the benefits that a programme generates relative to its costs, and may be computed using the following formula (Zappalà and Lyons, 2009):

$$\text{SROI} = \frac{\text{Net present value of benefits}}{\text{Net present value of inputs (investments)}}$$

Obtaining the values of the inputs (i.e., investments) is straightforward, as these are the data that the organization has on hand. For instance, input can be the contribution that the organization has put in to obtain food for children in the Child Aid scheme (e.g., $1,000) or the $10,000 paid to workers to work on a stipulated project or task. On the other hand, deriving the value for benefits is a complicated process, which requires details and computations as many assumptions are needed.

Hence, the value for benefits is not just the immediate outcome of the programme that one sees but requires the exclusion and subtraction of other factors. Therefore, it is necessary to examine the underlying assumptions in SROI, as the accuracy of the SROI ratio depends on the practicability of these assumptions. These assumptions are more important for forecast SROI, as compared to evaluative SROI. Upon meeting these assumptions, an equation to calculate the value of benefits may be obtained as follows (Teo, 2015; Zappalà and Lyons, 2009):

Benefits = Outcomes − Deadweight − Displacement − Attribution

1. *Deadweight*: In measuring deadweight, we like to know if the outcomes can be achieved even if the programme had never been implemented. To answer this question, we can look at the trend before the programme was implemented, whether there is already a pattern of data or a linear trajectory where the desired outcome will inevitably take place even in the absence of any intervention. Alternatively, we

can introduce a control group to see if there is a difference between those with and without programme intervention. This is often more difficult in practice due to ethical considerations.

2. *Displacement*: Has the current programme replaced another programme that would have resulted in the same or similar outcomes? Has the programme shifted the negative consequences to another area? If there is improvement in one particular area, but another location sufficed because the resources were diverted from one to another, then outcomes or benefits are simply displaced.

3. *Attribution*: Can the outcomes be attributed to other organizations contributions? For instance, at-risk youth might be staying in school more so due to the attention and care received by the staff and volunteers of one project, as compared to the free food provided to them by another organization. To answer this question, we need to consult stakeholders of other organizations, on top of analyzing other organizations' expenditures and outcomes.

In the next section, we will explore the seven principles of SROI, which are listed in Table 8 (Teo, 2015; Zappalà and Lyons, 2009).

Table 8.   Principles of Social Return on Investment.

No.	Principle of SROI	Elaboration on Principle
1	Involve stakeholders	Stakeholders should inform people about what is measured (and how it is measured and valued).
2	Understand what changes	Articulate how change is created and evaluate this through the evidence collected — this includes both positive and negative changes, as well as intended and unintended changes.
3	Value the things that matter	Use financial proxies so that the value of the outcomes can be recognized and accounted.
4	Only include what is material	Determine what information must be included in order to paint a true and fair picture so that stakeholders can draw reasonable conclusions.
5	Do not over-claim	Claim only the value that your organization is responsible for creating.
6	Be transparent	Demonstrate how the analysis may be considered accurate and honest.
7	Verify the result	Ensure appropriate independent verification.

Source: Zappalà and Lyons (2009, p. 21).

Apart from the definitions, benefits, critical assumptions, and principles of SROI, we need to be cognizant of the six steps of SROI analysis (Zappalà and Lyons, 2009). Refer to Table 9 on the SROI process and actions taken at each step.

We will explore SROI method in the context of the case study on WeCare@MarineParade. WeCare@MarineParade is a community intervention programme set up in Marine Parade, Singapore, with the goal of providing social services to 700 low-income households that were neglected under existing governmental assistance schemes (Kua *et al.*, 2017). WeCare has five strategic thrusts: (i) integrating last-mile solution, (ii) growing community assets, (iii) pioneering community solutions, (iv) building partnerships within and beyond Marine Parade, and (v) organizational excellence (Kua *et al.*, 2017). Table 10 shows a small subset of the SROI analysis conducted for WeCare@MarineParade.

To compute the SROI ratio, we need to obtain the aggregated social value and the total cost of intervention. In this example, after the removal of opportunity costs, the SROI ratio ranged between 1.25 and 1.97 (Kua *et al.*, 2017). In other words, for every $1 invested, WeCare was able to generate a social value of between $1.25 and $1.97 (Kua *et al.*, 2017). Hence, for every dollar spent in the WeCare@MarineParade programme, the social value generated via SROI analysis showed a greater output of benefit.

Table 9. SROI Process Steps.

No.	Step of SROI Process	Actions to be Taken
1	Establish scope + Identify key stakeholders	Identify what the SROI analysis will cover, who will be involved, and the nature of their involvement.
2	Map outcomes	Develop a theory of change that demonstrates how inputs, outputs, and outcomes are linked.
3	Evidence outcomes + Value outcome	Collect data that show if the outcomes have occurred and assign a monetary value to these outcomes.
4	Establish impact	Discount the impact of change that would have occurred naturally or is due to the impact of external factors.
5	Calculate the SROI	Add up the benefits, subtract the negatives, and compare the results with the investment made.
6	Report, use, and embed	Sharing the findings with stakeholders.

Source: Zappalà and Lyons (2009).

Table 10.　An Example of Social Impact Measure.

Activity	Input	Output	Outcome	Social Return (Benefits)
Social support via house visits	Time of volunteers (mostly free) and staff (minimal)	30-minute house visit bi-monthly	Greater life satisfaction	$238 to $541
Removal of hoarded items	Time of volunteers	One-time clearance	Reduce fire and health hazard and improved living conditions	$150
Refurbishment	Cost of materials	New coat of paint, new mattresses	Improved living conditions	$275 + $138

Source: Kua *et al.* (2017, pp. 104–106).

Just like all other methods of social impact measurement, SROI comes with its own limitations. Firstly, SROI is an extremely time- and resource-intensive undertaking, as one has to assign a monetary value to each activity or initiative the organization embarks on. Secondly, some important benefits and outcomes cannot be monetized, in which case assigning a monetary value may be a difficult task.

As mentioned earlier, the two methods, SROI and SAA, are similar. However, there are distinct differences between the two, with three key differences being purpose, valuation, and reporting (Gibbon and Dey, 2011). Regarding the purpose of evaluation, SAA is used to account for the past, whereas SROI can be used to account for the past in addition to forecasting purposes; on valuation, SAA does not require financial proxies but SROI requires comprehensive measures; finally, on reporting of evaluation, SAA audits must be made public, whereas SROI reports are recommended, but not made mandatory, for the public.

Conclusion

Measuring, reporting, and monitoring social impact pose a challenge to many social service organizations. While these organizations can choose from a range of methods to generate a comprehensive but precise and transparent measure of social impact, selecting the suitable one is not always straightforward (Miesing, n.d.).

Regardless of methodology, the quality of data matters. And it is up to the management to decide what form of data is most appropriate — both in terms of data reliability and the practical constraints to gaining access, such as the manpower and other resources needed to track programme activities, number of beneficiaries, and outcome measurement, to name a few.

Social impact evaluation is also a fine balance in resource allocation, managing stakeholders' expectations, and what is realistically feasible. For example, happiness and satisfaction are not only abstract sentiments but also highly subjective and may vary across cultures and communities. Social service organizations often find themselves under pressure to deliver support or services on the ground, and collecting evaluation data is often relegated to the background, not because it is unimportant, but because it is operationally challenging to manage both simultaneously. Lastly, programme impact evaluation is not a silver bullet to solve the problems and the challenges of social service organizations. Good governance and strategic directions matter, and evaluation is one of the tools to achieve the goal.

Bibliography

Bush, E. and Short, R. (2016). Mosquito nets are often used for fishing. A smart response is needed. *The Conversation.* Retrieved December 31, 2020 from https://theconversation.com/mosquito-nets-are-often-used-for-fishing-a-smart-response-is-needed-66283.

Carrington, D. (2018). Global use of mosquito nets for fishing 'endangering humans and wildlife'. *The Guardian.* Retrieved December 31, 2020 from https://www.theguardian.com/environment/2018/jan/31/global-use-of-mosquito-nets-for- fishing-endangering-humans-and-wildlife.

Future Learn. (n.d.). How and why to measure social impact. Retrieved September 8, 2021 from https://www.futurelearn.com/info/courses/social-enterprise-growing-a-sustainable-business/0/steps/20920.

Gibbon, J. and Dey, C. (2011). Developments in social impact measurement in the third sector: Scaling up or dumbing down? *Social and Environmental Accountability Journal,* 31(1), 63–72. DOI: 10.1080/0969160X.2011.556399.

Hanna, J. (2010). The hard work of measuring social impact. *Working Knowledge.* Retrieved December 31, 2020 from https://hbswk.hbs.edu/item/the-hard-work-of-measuring-social-impact.

Julien, D.A. (1997). The utilization of the logic model as a system level planning and evaluation device. *Evaluation and Program Planning*, 20(3), 251–257.

Karim, I. and Baker, D. (2014). All Saints Action Network Social Accounts (2011/2012). ASAN Social Accounting Working Group. Retrieved from https://www.asan.org.uk/wp-content/uploads/2014/10/ASAN-Social-Accounts-2011-2012.pdf.

Kua, Q.Q., Tang, O., and Lee, B. (2017). Social return on investment analysis of WeCare@MarineParade's network of aid. *Heartbeats: Journal of the Chua Thian Poh Community Leadership Programme*, 4. Retrieved from https://ctpclc.nus.edu.sg/wp- content/uploads/2017/05/Heartbeats-Vol4-Ch5.pdf.

Leong, C.H., Teng, E., and Ko, W. (2020). The state of ethnic congregation in Singapore today. In Leong, C.H. and Malone-Lee, L.C. (Eds.), *Building Resilient Neighbourhoods: The Convergence of Policies, Research, and Practice*, pp. 29–49. Singapore: Springer.

Miesing, P. (n.d.). Measuring social impact. Presentation. Albany, New York: School of Business, UAlbany-SUNY.

Nichols, P. (1999). *An Introduction to the Logframe Approach: Course Workbook & Materials*. Melbourne: IDSS.

Owens, B. (2019). People are using mosquito nets for fishing – and it works too well. *New Scientist*. Retrieved from https://www.newscientist.com/article/2222873-people-are-using-mosquito-nets-for-fishing-and-it-works-too-well/.

Teo, A. (2015). Running a social enterprise: Social return on investment (SROI). Presentation, AUN USR&S@Asia Engage Workshop.

Wee, A. (February 17, 1989). Racial limits set for HDB estates. *The Straits Times*.

Zappalà, G. and Lyons, M. (2009). Recent approaches to measuring social impact in the Third sector: An overview. *The Centre for Social Impact*.

Chapter 4

Board's Role in Financial Stewardship for Charities

Isabel Sim* and Ang Hao Yao†

**Department of Social Work, Faculty of Arts and Social Sciences,
National University of Singapore, Singapore*

†Chairman of Credit Counselling Singapore, Singapore

Introduction

The charity sector contributes value to society by enhancing the creation of a civil society with strong social and vibrant communities. Charities rely largely on donations from individuals and companies, and grants from government entities and other organizations, to fund their operations (Sim *et al.*, 2015). In turn, the charity's stakeholders, which include funders, donors, volunteers, and beneficiaries, expect the charity to be accountable and transparent in the way it utilizes the resources allocated to it.

A charity's Board of Directors is collectively responsible for ensuring that the charity is accountable and transparent. The charity's Board has the fiduciary duty of ensuring that financial reporting requirements are met, accounting and financial best practices are adhered to, and the charity maintains long-term financial sustainability by managing its reserves and investments effectively.

This chapter provides insight into the duties and responsibilities of a charity's Board of Directors in achieving good financial stewardship. It is divided into three sections.

Section 1: Compliance and financial reporting requirements for Charities in Singapore.
Section 2: Accounting and finance practices for Charities.
Section 3: Managing a Charity's Reserves and Investments.

Compliance and Reporting Requirements for Charities in Singapore

Legislative framework for charities in Singapore

In Singapore, charities must be registered with the Commissioner of Charities. Charities, as defined in the Charities Act, refer to organizations established exclusively for charitable purposes and they must conduct activities in furtherance of their charitable purposes which benefit the public.

All registered charities are automatically exempt from income tax. For properties that are used exclusively for charitable purposes, property tax may be exempted in full or partially upon application and reviewed by the Comptroller of Property Tax.

Institution of a Public Character (IPC) is a status accorded to a registered charity or an exempt charity for some time. Charities with the IPC status are required to conduct activities that exclusively benefit the local community and are not confined to sectional interests or groups of persons based on race, belief, or religion. IPCs are not allowed to conduct overseas activities that benefit the overseas community. IPCs are authorized to issue tax deduction receipts for qualifying donations received (National Council of Social Service Charity Portal, n.d.a).

All charities registered in Singapore are subject to legal and financial reporting requirements. Non-compliance may affect the charity's tax status and eligibility for grants. Specifically, they should comply with the Charities Act (1994) and Charities (Accounts and Annual Report) Regulations (2011). Besides the two legislations, charities also need to refer to the Code of Governance for Charities and Institutions of a Public Character (2023) for best practice guidelines. Table 1 shows a complete list of all the codes and regulations to comply with.

Table 1. List of Key Legislations and Guidelines for Charities in Singapore.

No.	Relevant Legislation for Charities	Source/Link
1.	Charities Act (1994)	Singapore Statutes Online, https://sso.agc.gov.sg/ Act/CA1994.
2.	Charities (Accounts and Annual Report) Regulations (2011)	Singapore Statutes Online, https://sso.agc.gov.sg/ SL/CA1994-S352-2011?DocDate=20180329.
3.	Code of Governance for Charities and IPC (2023)	Ministry of Culture, Community and Youth, Charity Portal, https://www.Charities.gov.sg/ Pages/Charities-and-IPCs/Manage-Your-Charity/Code-of-Governance-for-Charities-IPCs.aspx#.

Financial compliance and other reporting requirements

The Charities Act (1994) and Charities (Accounts and Annual Report) Regulations (2011) clearly state that all charities must keep accounting records and comply with financial reporting. Charities are required to submit documents to their regulators on a regular and ongoing basis. The list of required submissions is as follows:

1. Annual Submission to the Accounting and Corporate Regulatory Authority (ACRA) or the Registry Of Societies (ROS)
2. Annual Submissions to the Charity Portal
3. Annual Submissions to the Inland Revenue Authority of Singapore (IRAS)

Annual submission to the Accounting and Corporate Regulatory Authority (ACRA) or Registry of Societies (ROS)

Charities registered as a Company Limited by Guarantee (CLG) need to file their Annual Returns to ACRA, within seven months after the end of their Financial Year. The Annual Return consists of the Annual Report and audited Financial Statements for their last Financial Year.

If the charity is registered as a Society, it needs to file its Annual Return with ROS. Under the Societies Regulations, charities are required to submit their Annual Return within one month after the holding of their

Annual Report	**Financial Statements**
Online Financial Summary	**Governance Evaluation Checklist**

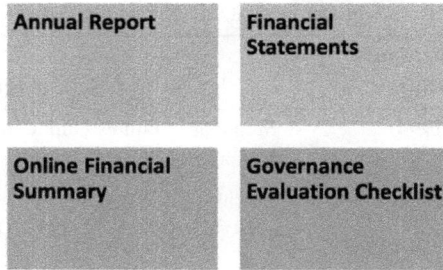

Fig. 1.   Summary of Important Annual Submissions Documents to the Charity Portal.
Source: Adapted from National Council of Social Service Charity Portal (2024).

Annual General Meeting (AGM), or if no meeting is held, once in every calendar year, within one month after the close of their financial year.

Annual submissions to the Charity portal

The Board should ensure that its charity has filed annual submissions to the Charity Portal on time. The Annual Submission documents include the Annual Report, audited Financial Statements, Online Financial Summary, and a Governance Evaluation Checklist.

The Annual Submission is to be submitted online via the Charity Portal within six months from the end of the financial year (Fig. 1). The documents are published on the Charity Portal for viewing by members of the public to promote transparency and accountability in the charity sector and facilitate informed giving (National Council of Social Service Charity Portal, n.d.b).

Annual submission to IRAS

For charities with IPC status, they are required to submit Tax-Deductible Donation records to IRAS electronically (Inland Revenue Authority, n.d.b). IPCs must submit all donation records received in the previous calendar year by 31st January annually.

According to the IRAS, charities are required to register for GST if the value of their taxable supplies exceeds S$1 million at the end of the calendar year, or at any point in time, the value of their taxable supplies is expected to exceed S$1 million in the next 12 months. This is even if they are engaged mostly in non-business activities (Inland Revenue Authority, n.d.a).

Role and responsibility of the Treasurer, Finance Committee, and Audit Committee

The Board must ensure that the organization meets legal and regulatory compliance requirements.

The Board's role includes establishing a competent Senior Management and Finance team as well as appointing the Treasurer, the Finance Committee, and the Audit Committee. The Management team, which comprises of CEO and CFO, supports the work of the Treasurer, Finance Committee and Audit Committee to ensure that charity meets legal and regulatory compliance.

The Code of Governance (2023) highlights that the Board should appoint a Treasurer, with a term limit of four consecutive years. The Terms of Reference of the Treasurer provide insight into a Treasurer's role and responsibilities. A sample is displayed in Fig. 2.

The Finance Committee oversees the charity's financial management, while the Audit Committee focuses on hiring as well as monitoring the performance of internal and external auditors who carry out internal audits and the annual financial audit. To avoid a conflict of interest, the Finance Committee Chair should not concurrently assume the role of an Audit Committee Chair. Ideally, all committee members should be equipped with relevant financial qualifications and work experience.

Figures 3 and 4 spell out the Terms of Reference for both the Audit Committee and the Finance Committee, respectively.

The Treasurer is expected to be a steward and fiduciary to the Charity. He or she typically has the following responsibilities:
   a. Assist the Board in fulfilling its responsibilities in directing the Charity to achieve its objectives, in compliance with ethical, legal and regulatory requirements
   b. Chair the Finance Committee (FC) and lead the FC in the fulfilment of its duties.
   c. Maintain oversight of a finance and accounting system and procedures, including procurement, receipting and payment processes.
   d. Establish strong checks and balances in the finance and accounting system to mitigate potential risks.
   e. Oversee financial sustainability and financial reporting of the Charity.
   f. Ensure that financial reporting is true and fair, in accordance with the relevant accounting standards, and completed/filed within the legal deadlines.

Fig. 2. Terms of Reference of Treasurer.

Source: Adapted from Board Appointment Guide for Charities 2021 (National Council of Social Services Charity Portal).

Finance Committee
  a. The Board shall establish a Finance Policy, with documented controls and procedures for financial matters in key areas, including procedures and controls in procurement, receipting, payment processes, as well as system for the delegation of authority and limits of approval in the Charity.
  b. The Board shall review and approve the capital and operating budgets and plans prepared by the management and regularly monitor the expenditure and outcomes of these plans.
  c. The Board shall monitor the financial status of the Charity and ensure financial sustainability required to carry on the Charity's activities for the long term. Where necessary, the Board shall review and approve financing options presented by the management.
  d. The Board shall ensure the proper accountability of funds and immediately address any financial irregularities or concerns.
  e. The Board shall ensure that Financial Reports are true and fair and contain adequate and necessary information for stakeholders.
  f. To oversee short and long-term investments, unless there is a separate investments committee.
  g. The Board must establish a Finance Committee (FC) to assist the Board in leading the finance agenda and other agenda defined by the charity.

Fig. 3.   Terms of Reference of Finance Committee.

Sources: Adapted from National Council of Social Services Charity Portal (2021a, 2021b).

Audit Committee
The Audit Committee's responsibilities include the following:
  a. To oversee the financial reporting and disclosure process, and monitor the choice of accounting policies and principles.
  b. To review the audit plans and reports of the external auditors and internal auditors, and considers the effectiveness of the actions taken by management on the auditors' recommendations.
  c. To conduct periodic internal checks on key processes to ensure compliance with the established procedures, and report to the Board on the findings and recommendations for improvements.
  d. To analyse and address the risks that are associated with the key processes.
  e. To oversee regulatory compliance and whistleblower guidelines (where applicable)
  f. To report to the Board of any financial irregularities, concerns and opportunities.
  g. To liaise with auditors on any significant matters arising.

Fig. 4.   Terms of Reference for Audit Committee.

Source: Adapted from National Council of Social Services Charity Portal (2021b).

Accounting and Finance for Charity

Once the Treasurer, the Audit Committee, and Finance Committee are appointed, the Board must put in place accounting and financial policies and practices for the charity's accountability and long-term financial sustainability. The areas of focus for charity accounting and finance are as follows:

1. Good account record-keeping and up-to-date accounting and finance policies.
2. Long-term financial sustainability through budgeting, financial planning, and ongoing financial reviews.

Good account record-keeping and up-to-date accounting and finance policies

The Board must establish the charity's key accounting and finance policies, with input from the auditors and the charity's Finance Team. The Board must have access to accurate and up-to-date accounting and financial information since they are responsible for making decisions that will affect the charity's operations. Once the accounting and finance policies are put in place, the Senior Management, together with the finance staff team, can prepare and provide accurate, consistent, and timely Financial Reports for the Finance Committee's review.

Good record-keeping by the staff team is essential

Good record-keeping is fundamental, as the accounting information is required for the charity's budgeting, financial planning, and preparation of Financial Reports. The Charity's accounting and finance practices need to be updated with the latest regulations. Care must be taken to ensure the charity's Financial Reports are true and fair, providing information for stakeholders in an accountable and transparent manner. In particular, donors and funders who provide funding to charities, will require the charities to keep proper records and audited accounts.

Accounting and finance policies for the Charity

The Board must establish appropriate accounting and finance policies, such as the Revenue Recognition Principle and Expense Recognition Principle, as they serve as the bedrock for the entire accounting framework in ensuring accuracy, consistency, and transparency in the financial statements. Other important accounting and finance policies specific to charities in Singapore, include the Procurement policy, Fundraising

Efficiency Ratio (FER), Anti-Money Laundering (AML), and Countering the Financing of Terrorism (CFT) policy.

As the charity's main sources of income are from public funds, it is important for the charity to establish its procurement policy to outline how the Charity manages its purchase of goods and services to ensure fairness and transparency. For larger procurements, it is recommended that a Tender Committee be set up to evaluate submissions to ensure fairness, transparency, and accountability in the process of awarding contracts.

In Singapore, all charities and IPCs are expected to keep their Fundraising Efficiency Ratio (FER) below 30%. This is commonly known as the 30/70 rule. The FER shows how much net income a charity generates for every dollar spent on fundraising. Essentially, it measures how cost-effective the charity is at raising money. This requirement ensures that charities are prudent in planning and executing their fundraising campaigns.

Another important finance policy, regulated by law in Singapore, is the Anti-Money Laundering (AML) and Countering the Financing of Terrorism policy (CFT). Staff should be trained to identify red flags and there should be a process for the filing of a Suspicious Transaction Report to the Suspicious Transaction Reporting Office.

Besides the Accounting and Finance policies, the Finance Committee needs to put in place accounting and finance work procedures such as controls and procedures in procurement, receipting, payment processes, as well as a system for the delegation of authority and financial limits of approval.

Long-term financial sustainability through budgeting, financial planning and ongoing financial reviews

The Finance Committee is tasked by the Board to oversee the charity's budgeting and financial planning. The Finance Committee works closely with Senior Management and the finance team by reviewing the budgets prepared and presenting these financial proposals to the Board for approval. The budgeting process is carried out annually, usually with two to four reviews during the Financial Year. Budget modifications may be necessary during the Financial Year should there be changes in the priorities or operating environment.

The Finance Committee monitors the organization's financial status by meeting regularly with the Senior Management and finance team to examine Financial Statements and check on the expenditure and outcomes, including forecasting and planning for future income and expenses. The Committee is constantly comparing actual financial performance against the budget and investigating significant variances.

At the Board meetings, the Finance Committee communicates significant financial matters that require the Board's attention. The Finance Committee determines the contents of the Financial Reports and how often these updates should be shared and reviewed. Generally, the Financial Reports highlight key information about the charity's cash and financial position, resource allocation, budget adherence, and any donor-imposed contribution restrictions. Important aspects of the charity's operation, like revenues, expenses, budgeted vs. actual amounts, and cash flows, should be regularly verified.

As not all Board members may be financially trained, the Finance Committee needs to explain the Financial Reports and the implications of the financial decisions (Visram, 2022). This will help the charity's Board in understanding financial trends, risks, and expected outcomes better so they can develop informed strategies for handling financial changes or setbacks as part of their oversight function.

Ultimately, the Board is responsible for ensuring that the charity is financially sustainable in the long run. They must monitor the charity's operations and financial performance to ensure that they are aligned with the charity's strategic goals.

To achieve long-term financial sustainability, the Board works with the Senior Management to develop multi-year budgets that support the long-term strategic plans (Visram, 2022). For example, many charities set long-term financial goals such as building up working capital, cash reserves, or capital budgets to fund purchases of equipment, as part of long-term financial planning. Hence, it is a good practice for charities to have a three-year or five-year budget forecast, so that they can achieve their organization's strategic goals.

Reserve and Investment for Charities' Long-Term Financial Sustainability

Introduction to the Charity's reserves and the role of the Board

Another major area of financial duty and responsibility for the Board is to manage the charity's reserves and investments. Charities are encouraged

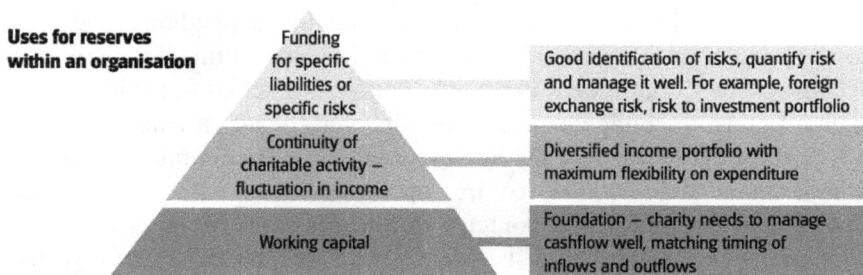

Fig. 5.   Method for Determining Reserves.

Source: Adapted from Sayer Vincent (2012).

to generate surplus, to build up their reserves and in turn invest their reserves, as part of their long-term financial sustainability strategy.

Determining reserves level

A charity's reserves act as a financial buffer to cover unexpected expenses and maintain operations during difficult times or invest in future projects. Without a reserves policy, charities may run the risk of having funds gradually depleted over time and not being available when they need the funds (Nonprofits Assistance Fund, 2021). If the charity is below its target reserves, the Board should take steps to raise the reserves by increasing income or reducing expenses. If the charity is above its target, it should explain the need for the excess reserves.

Though there is no consensus among charities as to the appropriate level of reserves to maintain, the National Council of Social Services (NCSS) recommends that charities should carry out thorough analyses of income and expenditures, risk profiles, as well as past and future financial trends to develop their own reserves policy (National Council of Social Service Charity Portal, 2021). An approach in determining the charity's reserve is summarized in Fig. 5.

Types of reserves

A charity's reserves are classified into two categories: the Unrestricted Reserves and the Restricted Reserves.

Unrestricted Reserves are essentially the cumulative amount of retained earnings that can be used for any purpose deemed appropriate by the Board to further the charity's mission. It is common practice for charities to maintain Unrestricted Reserves equivalent to at least one year of operating budget. It is the Board's responsibility to build up its Unrestricted Reserves. This allows the charity to be financially resilient, maintain adequate working capital, and be better positioned to manage its operations sustainably. There should be emergency cash to cover shortfall whenever there is a dip in income.

Restricted Reserves are donations or grants given to a charity for a specific purpose set by the donor or funder. The charity can only use these funds towards the funder's or donor's intent. Examples of Restricted Reserves include (i) a Building Fund where donations are collected to purchase or develop a building, (ii) an Endowment Fund where the fund is invested and the investment income can be used for a specified purpose, or (iii) Restricted Income and Expenses for programmes funded by the government ministry, e.g., Ministry of Health or Ministry of Education.

Developing the reserves policy

A charity's Reserves policy should be aligned with its strategic goals and operational sustainability. A communication strategy for explaining the charity's Reserves to the public needs to be established (Australian Charities and Not-for-Profits Commission, n.d.). Key disclosure items include why the charity needs to have reserves and a clear explanation for how the charity determines its appropriate level of Reserves. There should be a process for reviewing the level of reserves, a strategy for building and maintaining reserves, and authorization for the use of reserves. For reserves that are not needed in the near term, it should be invested to generate returns that can be used to fund the charity's operations.

Charities are required to establish and disclose their reserves policy in their Annual Report and Financial Statement (National Council of Social Service Charity Portal, 2017). See Fig. 6 for details.

Introduction to Charity's investments and the role of the Board

Charities may invest their reserves to provide financial returns that can be utilized to further the Charity's mission. To fulfil their fiduciary duty in managing the charity's financial assets, the Board needs to understand and apply the "Prudent Man Rule" ("Harvard College v. Amory," 1830). The

RESERVES MANAGEMENT

• The charity should maintain some level of reserves to ensure its long-term financial sustainability.

• The charity should develop a reserves policy and **disclose its reserves policy** in its annual report [NOTE: This is a legislative requirement for charities with gross annual receipts or total expenditure of $500,000 and above, and all IPCs.]

• The charity should ensure that **restricted funds** and **endowment funds** are set up solely for clear and justifiable needs.

The charity should make sure that these funds are used or transferred to other funds only after getting the permission of the donor to do so.

The charity must inform prospective donors of the:
- Purpose of the funds; and
- Amount of funds needed.

For existing restricted and endowment funds, the charity must disclose the **purpose, size** and **planned timing of use** for these funds.

• If the charity invests its reserves, it should do so in accordance with an **investment policy** approved by the Board. It should also obtain advice from **qualified professional advisors** if deemed necessary by the Board.

Fig. 6.   Pointers on Reserve Management.

Source: Adapted from the Code of Corporate Governance for Charity and IPC (2017).

Prudent Man Rule serves as a general guideline for the Board that is managing the assets on behalf of the charity. Under the rule, the Board has a fiduciary duty to invest as a "prudent man" like investing his own assets, bearing in mind the needs of the beneficiaries, the need for capital preservation, as well as the amount and regularity of income.

In Singapore, the Investment Committee, which is made up of experienced investment professionals, is appointed by the Board to manage the charity's investments. It needs to refer to the charity's Investment Policy Statement (IPS) and ensure that the investment strategy is aligned with the Charity's investment objectives, risk tolerance, and time horizon.

Developing Charity's Investment Policy Statement

An Investment Policy Statement (IPS) is designed to address the objectives, constraints, unique circumstances, and overall oversight procedures that govern the investment-related activities of a charity. A good IPS should clearly state the responsibilities of all parties involved in managing

---

Elements of a clearly defined investment policy statement
  1. Purpose and scope
  2. Definition of duties
  3. Objectives and circumstances
  4. Strategic asset allocation framework
  5. Rebalancing
  6. Liquidity policy
  7. Spending policy
  8. Risk management
  9. Responsible investing
  10. Unique circumstances
  11. Monitoring and review process

Fig. 7. Elements of Clearly Defined IPS.

Source: Adapted from Coffey and Lato (2011).

the charity's investments. The financial objectives within the context of how much risk the charity is willing and able to bear will be disclosed, and long-term strategic asset allocations are specified. Lastly, the IPS should set forth operational guidelines and rules for monitoring and reviewing all facets of the investment (Coffey and Lato, 2011). A summary on the elements of a clearly defined IPS is displayed in Fig. 7.

Investment Committee — Role and responsibilities

The Investment Committee needs to refer to the charity's IPS for guidelines and procedures in managing the charity's investments. They need to consider the types of investment instruments that is suitable for the charity's risk–return profile, cashflow requirements, and exit strategy.

To begin, the Investment Committee needs to examine the charity's risk–return profile, and cashflow requirements. Does the charity need to maintain a high liquidity level? Or can the charity take on more risk, with a longer-term investment period? Another important step for the Investment Committee is to find out if there are any prohibited investments. For example, there are charities restricting investments in industries like smoking or gambling.

With a clear understanding of the charity's risk–return profile, cashflow requirements, and restrictions on investments (if any), the Investment Committee is better positioned to determine the types of asset class (Debt vs. Equity) and investment instruments that they may invest in and how these funds would be allocated. Fixed Deposits, Bonds, or equity are good examples. Some charities invest only in fixed deposits and treasury bills, while others invest in a portfolio with global bonds and equity.

A risk management framework and preferably a defined stop-loss threshold should be implemented for the purpose of capital preservation. More importantly, an exit strategy for a charity must be in place, taking into consideration the length of the process it will take to liquidate its investments.

A licensed Fund Management Company may be appointed to manage the charity's investment. The Investment Committee's role is to appoint a licensed investment advisor or manager. They review the investment proposals presented by the licensed investment management company and monitor the investment performance at least once a year or as and when the investment losses reach a defined stop-loss threshold. During the periodic reporting by the investment management company, the Investment Committee needs to decide if the investment should be withdrawn, reallocated, or maintained at the status quo.

With proper understanding of the types of reserves, the need and level of reserves and how to manage them, charities can better ensure the sustainability of their organization and programmes. The Board needs to pay close attention to ensure that surplus are invested in financial instruments that are approved in the charity's Investment Policy Statement (IPS).

Conclusion

We conclude this chapter by summarizing the topics presented. We covered the framework for compliance and financial reporting requirements for charities in Singapore. We highlighted the Board's duties and responsibilities in managing the charity's accounting and financial reporting practices, and emphasized the need to maintain accounting and financial records, policies, and procedures that adhered to the industry's best practices and guidelines. Lastly, the Board plays a key role in ensuring the charity maintains long-term financial sustainability by managing its reserves and investments. Most importantly, the Charities must ensure that there is a pipeline of Board members with finance and investment skills, and experience in managing charity accounting, to ensure that the charity stays financially sustainable. Without the qualified board members to discharge these responsibilities, the charities will not be progressive.

Acknowledgements

We would like to thank Yeo Zuoheng Khalispel for his assistance with this research paper.

Bibliography

Australian Charities and Not-for-Profits Commission (n.d.). Charity Reserves: Financial Stability and Sustainability. Australian Government. https://www.acnc.gov.au/tools/guides/charity-reserves-financial-stability-and-sustainability.

Coffey, G. and Lato, M.B. (2011). Investment Policy Statement: Elements of a Clearly Defined IPS for Non-Profits. R. Investments. https://russellinvestments.com/-/media/files/us/insights/institutions/non-profit/elements-of-a-clearly-defined-ips-for-non-profits-an-update.pdf.

Harvard College v. Amory, 26 Mass. (9 Pick.) 446 446 (Supreme Judicial Court of Massachusetts 1830).

Inland Revenue Authority (n.d.a). Charities and Non-Profit Organisations. https://www.iras.gov.sg/taxes/goods-services-tax-(gst)/specific-business-sectors/charities-and-non-profit-organisations.

Inland Revenue Authority (n.d.b). Submission of Donation Records. https://www.iras.gov.sg/digital-services/others/institutions-of-a-public-character-and-qualifying-grantmakers/submission-of-donation-records.

National Council of Social Service Charity Portal (2017). Code of Governance for Charities and IPCs. https://www.charities.gov.sg/Pages/Charities-and-IPCs/Manage-Your-Charity/Code-of-Governance-for-Charities-IPCs.aspx#.

National Council of Social Service Charity Portal (2021). Reserves Policy Guide for Charities. https://www.charities.gov.sg/PublishingImages/Resource-and-Training/Guides-Templates-Awards/Guides/Documents/Reserves%20Policy%20Guide%20for%20Charities.pdf.

National Council of Social Service Charity Portal (2024, 26 January). Guide on Preparing Annual Submissions. https://www.charities.gov.sg/PublishingImages/Resource-and-Training/Guides-Templates-Awards/Guides/Documents/Preparing%20Annual%20Submissions.pdf.

National Council of Social Service Charity Portal (n.d.a). About IPCs. https://www.charities.gov.sg/Pages/Charities-and-IPCs/IPCs/About-IPCs.aspx#.

National Council of Social Service Charity Portal (n.d.b). Annual Submission. https://www.charities.gov.sg/Pages/Charities-and-IPCs/Manage-Your-Charity/Annual-Submissions.aspx#.

National Council of Social Services Charity Portal (2021a). Board Appointment Guide for Charities. https://www.charities.gov.sg/PublishingImages/Resource-and-Training/Guides-Templates-Awards/Guides/Documents/Board%20Appointment%20Guide%20for%20Charities.pdf.

National Council of Social Services Charity Portal (2021b). Board Committees and Terms of Reference (by SSI). https://www.charities.gov.sg/Publishing Images/Resource-and-Training/Guides-Templates-Awards/SOP-and-Templates/Documents/Sample_TORs_Board_Committees.pdf.

Nonprofits Assistance Fund (2021). Operating Reserves with Nonprofit Policy Examples. https://propelnonprofits.org/resources/operating-reserves-with-nonprofit-policy-examples/.

Sayer Vincent (2012). Beyond Reserves: How Charities Can Make Their Reserves Work Harder. ACEVO, Charity Finance Group & Institute of Fundraising. https://www.sayervincent.co.uk/wp-content/uploads/2021/08/BeyondReserves.pdf.

Sim, I., Ghoh, C., Loh, A., and Chiu, M. (2015). The Social Service Sector in Singapore an Exploratory Study on the Financial Characteristics of Institutions of a Public Character (IPCs) in the Social Service Sector. https://www.charities.gov.sg/PublishingImages/Resource-and-Training/Publications/Books/Documents/NUS_CSDA_The%20Social%20Service%20Sector%20In%20Singapore%202015.pdf.

Singapore Statutes Online (2011). Charities (Accounts and Annual Report) Regulations. https://sso.agc.gov.sg/SL/CA1994-S352-2011?DocDate=20180329.

Visram, O. (2022, August 12). Six Key Responsibilities of the Non-Profit Finance Committee. Enkel. https://www.enkel.ca/blog/not-for-profit/key-nonprofit-finance-committee-responsibilitiee-responsibilities/.

Chapter 5

Some Challenges in Managing Volunteers and Enhancing Their Participation in the Social Service Sector in Singapore[*]

S. Vasoo

Department of Social Work, National University of Singapore, Singapore

Introduction

There are quite a number of social and voluntary welfare organizations still take a lacklustre approach in managing and promoting the participation of volunteers who are more often than not seen as an organizational appendage, being viewed as a burden to the staff and a spent force that does not generate but consumes more organizational resources. Such a myopic viewpoint cannot go unchallenged as efforts of professional manpower can be more effective when complemented by volunteers who bring the human dimension to the delivery of social services. In all human miseries and needs, both professionals and volunteers are required to find the most meaningful and cost-effective way towards human development and problem-solving. It is becoming noticeable that many agencies in the social and welfare sectors are outsourcing their services to service

---

[*]This chapter was originally published in S. Vasoo (2019). Developing Volunteers for the Social Service Sector. NUS Social Work Department. (Chapter 3), pp. 43–67.

contractors and this can retard volunteerism, especially when we need to tamper communities to be less utilitarian and materialistic in extending social care and help for those in need (Rothschild *et al.*, 2016).

Volunteerism in the social service sector is focused more on task-centered community activities, which mainly cover short-term projects involving socio-educational and recreational activities. Consequently, volunteer groups have gravitated to become task- or programme-centered. This is further reinforced by the outsourcing of community services to the private sector, which has been contracted to deliver services or activities. The consequences of such an approach can reinforce the learned helplessness of the beneficiaries who are usually relegated to passive or dependent roles.

Participation of volunteers has undergone significant transformation in the last few years as activities of clan and lineage organizations (Esman, 1978; Seah, 1973; Vasoo, 1991) have declined despite recent efforts to encourage them to reform and rejuvenate. In response to this situation, more formal voluntary social and welfare organizations have been and are being established to assist the disadvantaged sector of Singapore's community, such as the disabled and sick, aged destitute, individuals and families in distress, and children and youths in need of care and guidance. Also, neighbourhood betterment activities undertaken by Residents' Committees (RCs) in the public housing estates have increased pointedly in the last decade (Sundblom *et al.*, 2016). The government's conscious policies in avoiding the welfarist model and emphasis on promoting self-help through the provision of tax-exempt status, matching grant, land, and capital cost for selected voluntary social and welfare organizations have contributed to the growth of voluntary efforts involving many helping hands to care for the unfortunate and less-abled citizens.

Addressing Volunteer Participation Issues

The observation that volunteerism participation in social services has become highly task-oriented, focussing on short-term projects, many of which are outsourced, has negatively affected volunteer participation in general. Such an orientation or drive is likely to dampen if not reduce volunteer commitment and motivation to help social service and welfare agencies tackle prevailing community problems as well as emerging social issues and needs. In the long run, the spirit of community service and volunteerism will be eroded and each man will only care for himself and the axiom "all men are brothers" will end as each will only care for his own. This will lead to the rise of uncaring Singaporeans, making our society socially unhealthy (Nesbit *et al.*, 2016).

Consequences of increase in outsourcing activities on volunteerism

It is noticed that there is an increasing trend by agencies to outsource community activities. Why is this the case? In the name of efficiency and the urgency for a quick turnover, agencies often face time constraints. Therefore, most community activities are planned within a short time frame and often tied to the term of office holders. Such an emphasis can make volunteer groups insular and not development-oriented. They then become task- or activity-centered, slowly digressing from being people-centered, which aims to promote self-help and community ownership in those who are beneficiaries of the community activities. As such, many social and voluntary organizations adopt a less outreaching approach to understand the changing needs of the community. In the longer term, such a move will make them more detached rather than keeping in touch with the needs of people or the client groups who are uninvolved or are vulnerable to social problems (Wiarda *et al.*, 2016).

Effects of centralization of leadership and population ageing on volunteerism

The leadership or management of social and voluntary sectors is generally left to a small group of elected office bearers who bear the responsibilities. Such a de-facto style of management can lead to leadership centralization. As such, the burdens of delivering community activities or not-for-profit projects are carried by a small group of organizational leaders who will eventually be affected by compassion fatigue. More often than not, the leadership of the organizations in the social service sector does not rejuvenate, and those in leadership stay entrenched for many terms as there are few younger members or others who are prepared to step into the positions, despite them wanting to give way. Somehow, the old leaders in the management circles continue, and they then become the domineering force, with the leadership becoming centralized in the hands of a few seniors who continue year in and year out to run the outfit in their old traditional or conservative style. To avert this situation, more attention should be devoted by the leadership to encourage and enlist more resourceful and interested people to head different service projects to deal with community needs and concerns. To help a smoother transition of leadership in the sector, it will be prudent for volunteer leaders in the organization's board to implement an orderly change by inducting younger leaders to take a lead in the delivery of services which will meet new emerging social needs. The issue of succession of leadership faced by many organizations in the social service sector will be addressed, provided appropriate steps are taken by incumbent boards, which can sometimes be rather exclusive and protective of their turf. In the near future, the number of young volunteers will decline, and this will affect the work of voluntary social and welfare organizations, which rely on younger volunteers for active programmes. This is because one of the most significant social phenomena facing Singapore in the immediate decade is population ageing. The population ageing trend has become conspicuous. In 1990, there were about 118,300 persons aged 60 years and above, and by the tum of the year 2014, the number increased to 431,601 persons (Department of Statistics, 2014; Yap and Gee, 2015). It is estimated that there will be about 900,000 elderly, i.e., about 25% of Singaporeans will be above 60 years, by the year 2030. The pool of younger adults available to be tapped for volunteers will drop dramatically because our population growth is dropping due to a lower fertility rate below the replacement standing at about 1.5 persons. This serious drop below the replacement rate will create socio-economic consequences, such as lack of manpower to produce goods and services and more importantly the availability of younger persons to provide care and support for the community of older people and families with seniors. The young will be so stretched in supporting older family members that they will not be able to participate in voluntary services, as they will have less discretionary time at their disposable than their counterparts in the preceding generation, who faced less time constraints and had more manpower to be enlisted as volunteers for altruistic activities. However, the reduction of young volunteers could be augmented by mobilizing older persons, who will form the potential pool for volunteer manpower. Currently, few organizations have a comprehensive plan for tapping the rich experience and expertise of our retired senior citizens. It is therefore desirable for organizations to identify various voluntary activities for their involvement (Sundblom *et al.*, 2016).

Low participation rate and demand for volunteers' limited spare time

It is observed that the rate of participation of volunteers, particularly young adults, is not significant and this could be due to the less tangible benefits to be gained directly by them from volunteering in community service programmes. The high participation of volunteers and beneficiaries is critical in ensuring the sustainability of community activities for community problem-solving. Besides this issue, the social and voluntary sector must promote more concrete services to meet the beneficiaries' social and economic needs, as this will address the public goods dilemma and reduce the cost of participation. When volunteer groups and organizations do not bear this in mind in their community service, both minorities and working-class households will not be motivated to participate in some mainstream community projects such as literacy education, matched savings, environmental protection, provision of shelter, provision of sanitation, credit unions and co-operatives, potable and clean water, early childhood learning, infant and maternal healthcare, and preventive healthcare, vaccination, retirement planning, eldercare, and vocational training.

However, with improvements in working conditions, Singaporeans have more leisure time. At least 50% of working Singaporeans have about 14 hours of leisure time per week. This can be tapped by various social and welfare organizations. As leisure time is limited, Singaporeans are less likely to expend it in voluntary activities, which are beneficial and useful (Olson, 1965; Smith *et al.*, 2016). It is therefore important for voluntary social and welfare organizations to make their voluntary service programmes interesting, attractive, and appealing for volunteers. Unless this is actively considered, they will not be able to attract and sustain volunteers. It has been found that organizations which offer mundane and routine voluntary service programmes cannot sustain the interest of volunteers longer than necessary (Gidron, 1983; Goh *et al.*, 2015). The participation of volunteers in Singapore's voluntary social and welfare services is still rather low. It has been found that only 6% of the population between 15 and 55 years of age is involved in voluntary work. This participation rate compares less favourably to other countries such as the United States of America, Japan, and the United Kingdom, where the participation rates are 39%, 25% and 12%, respectively. The participation rate in all countries, including Singapore, will probably decline in the near future, and this will affect the work of voluntary social and welfare organizations, which rely more on younger volunteers who face competing demands for their time. Robotic technology will undertake work that is normally assigned to volunteers.

Implications of lack of coordination in service learning and hollowing out of volunteerism talents

Another significant issue that social service institutions have to address is the lack of concerted effort to coordinate the many sprouting volunteer groups and voluntary organizations that provide community services. At the same time, these heart-string organizations have to compete with more lucrative and highly incentivized service exchange programmes and business and research projects. As a result, there is a hollowing out of the more resourceful younger volunteer talents from the setups promoting philanthropic and community activities. In recent years, many businesses and large multinational corporations have provided very attractive internships to employable young adults for work attachment, and this siphons off many younger persons from tertiary institutions and social service sectors, which tend to offer fewer perks and incentives to engage them in service projects. These competing opportunities are becoming a reality. Therefore, the attraction of young volunteer talents away from the social service sector is unavoidable but the challenge for the social service sector is to design more innovative projects to draw younger volunteer talents to participate in community problem solving activities which can provide special intrinsic satisfaction for which monetary compensation cannot. A well-coordinated and challenging resource bank for service and learning innovative projects, where both young and adult volunteers can get access and make a good informed choice where they can be attached for a period of time to implement their prospective projects, is one way ahead. However, the older urban neighbourhoods are seeing a draining of the more capable who are resourceful, worsening the situation with less able manpower to tackle the problems of the community. This being the situation, there will be limited good volunteer manpower to be mobilized for community problem-solving (Berger et al., 2016).

Effects of inflexible volunteering and lack of opportunities for innovation

Over the years, it has been observed that the social service sector has grown, and in some cases, many agencies have become mega-organizations which have developed rules and regulations to manage staff and volunteers in delivering services to their consumers. Volunteer tasks become more rule-bound and the volunteering schedules are arranged for the convenience of paid personnel and not for tapping the volunteer manpower to meet the requirements of social service organizations. Therefore, this strait-laced approach does not help to harness more volunteers who are responsive to flexible volunteering, and this is more suitable for those volunteers whose talents can be enlisted for innovative projects. Increasingly, many professionals are involved in globalized jobs and their professional expertise in such areas as management, marketing, branding, fundraising, initiating sustainable social enterprises, and data analytics can be garnered for philanthropic and voluntary activities. The Social Service sector will have to be less rigid in tapping a vast potential pool of volunteers who are skilled and capable of adding value to the work of the sector, which will ultimately lose out by remaining insular and unresponsive to the changing globalized work world. Also, more attempts must be made by the sector to encourage and enable professionals to have more opportunities to pilot community service projects, which entail innovative ideas in services to meet the needs of various disadvantaged and marginalized groups together with social and community workers. A wider and varied volunteer pool can help to accommodate diverse individual volunteers who will help the sector become more effective in community problem-solving.

Some Steps to Enhance Volunteer Management and Participation

In meeting some challenges confronting community development, it is proposed for key leaders to consider involving younger volunteers in community problem solving, community betterment projects and assist in the promotion of social enterprises to enhance community development efforts in the various country settings (Smith *et al.*, 2016).

Need for setting up volunteers management and development center

Currently, there are community volunteer activities or service learning activities that are not well coordinated with many activities are fractured and disjointed, leading to the poor involvement of students. Recently, some tertiary educational institutions began paying more attention to service learning. However, inadequate resources are still being deployed to give credence to the importance of community service learning to imbue social responsibility in the young and promote corporate social responsibility among institutions of higher learning. More serious efforts must be made to promote philanthropic passion in the young, and it will help our society to have more individuals who can lead and inspire others to be involved in community betterment and public good activities. To help drive and build philanthropic activities in tertiary educational institutions, a Centre for Philanthropic Activities can be established to recruit, train, promote and sustain philanthropic efforts. This will have to be a fully fledged center run on a non-profit basis.

Enhancing self-help and community ownership

In carrying out community service activities, there should be fewer outsourcing contracts and more in-sourcing activities by mobilizing students to form not-for-profit organizations or social enterprises. Such attempts will provide more opportunities for student volunteer groups and beneficiaries to participate in decision-making so that they all can take ownership. Community care groups and support networks can be formed. This will make beneficiaries not passive recipients of services but rather engaged in problem-solving. Student volunteer groups and organizations can widen the base of participation by helping to form various interest groups or task forces to work on various social issues and projects, such as security watch and crime prevention, co-operative care services, improvements to recreational facilities, pollution control, thrift through micro-credit groups, and environmental enhancement projects. It will be useful, where possible, to encourage beneficiaries to take charge in finding more effective ways to deal with local matters possibly with the support of the local councils. This will truly promote community development as local residents or beneficiaries will learn and find more realistic solutions to solve their specific needs and problems and become accountable for their decisions. However, with the move towards information technology, people could become impersonal and more homebound, social interactions could be reduced, and social bonding could be threatened. Therefore, online contact has to be complemented by more personalized outreach efforts.

Implications of leadership rejuvenation and organizational renewal to volunteerism

It is also observed that a significant number of grassroots leaders of community organizations in the mature housing estates are above 50 years of age. These organizations face difficulties in recruiting younger residents to take up leadership (Vasoo, 1994). With the greying of the organizational leadership, there is an urgency to rejuvenate the leadership of community organizations by attracting younger student talents to participate in them. It is not just sufficient to recruit them, but they must be mentored by committed older leaders. With attachment to specific mentors, student volunteers can be anchored to the organizations, and this will reduce attrition among those taking up leadership in organizations dominated by seniors. A rejuvenated leadership will continue to be vibrant and relevant to meet the needs and aspirations of the younger generation. We must also attract younger people-centered volunteers and potential leaders who can be given all the support to carry out community problem-solving activities. People-centered volunteers and leaders are proactive, and they should not be piled with so many tasks that they then suffer burnout. More importantly, volunteers should be given management skills training to understand the needs of the beneficiaries so that they can help make community organizations responsive to tackling emerging social needs (Colomy *et al.*, 1987; Gidron, 1983). It is crucial for each social and welfare organization to set up a Volunteer Management and Development Centre which will recruit, train, deploy, develop, and recognize volunteers. Aggregation Information Technology (IT) can be put in place to match volunteers in terms of their service offer to those people in need of service or help.

Volunteering to reach out to lower-income residents and minorities

As many countries have an open economy and are becoming more global-ized, it is inevitable that people with low skills are likely to face depressed wages, and this can lead to a widening income gap (Goh, 2000; Goh *et al.*, 2015). People with better skills are likely to move ahead, while those with low skills and lower literacy in information technology will fall behind in income. Social stratification based on socio-economic classes confounded by ethnicity may surface if excessive free market competition is not tempered. As a consequence, social conflicts could emerge, and when this is capitalized by political and racial fanatics, community harmony and cohesion could be fractured (Lee, 2000). As such, student groups and organizations, including community organizations, can take preventive measures to deliver community-based self-help programmes, such as social and educational assistance, computer training, educational head start for children of low-income families, child care services, youth vocational guidance and counselling programmes, family life and development activities, and continuing learning programmes to help the socially disadvantaged groups. As a long-term measure for people-capability building, it is important for us to develop more educational head start projects for low-income children in the nursery age group. The increase of such projects through community partnership of various self-help groups, unions, co-operatives and not-for-profit organizations will help children from disadvantaged backgrounds level up and acquire productive skills for their future livelihood. Matched savings schemes tied up with such projects can be initiated. These community development efforts can help to reduce the social friction between classes and ethnic groups. Fanatics will find it less tempting to exploit the race card as the problems facing low-income families cut across all ethnic group. So, the realistic solution is to help level up the capabilities of all disadvantaged children regardless of their ethnicity.

Impact of renewal and rejuvenation of ageing neighbourhoods on volunteering

It will be evident that in the next two decades, we will see a number of silver neighbourhoods. If attempts by policymakers to renew and rejuvenate these neighbourhoods are slower than population ageing in these places, then these neighbourhoods will become listless and socially rundown. Local social and economic activities will slow down, and younger people will not find these neighbourhoods attractive to live in as they will be dominated by senior citizens. Ultimately, there will be more families facing the need for care of elderly parents or relatives. As many of these families have working family members, they will face the burden of care. Social breakdowns are likely without accessible social support and community care services delivered at the local level. Therefore, there will be a demand for more community-based programmes to cater to the needs of families who have frail-aged family members. The number of such families is expected to increase in the next decade. In light of this situation, student volunteer groups and voluntary welfare organizations, together with the involvement of residents as well as hospitals, will have to work as partners to provide community care services such as home help, meal services, daycare, integrated housing, and community nursing. Here, community care co-operatives could be formed to offer services which will be more convenient and accessible to families with frail elderly needing care and attention. There is potential for this type of social enterprise to be established with the families as one of the stakeholders. Here, student groups with medical and other professional training have a role to play in community social and health betterment.

Volunteering in early intervention educational and parenting programmes

Volunteers can play a significant role in early educational intervention and parenting programmes. Educational mentoring schemes for young children from working-class and marginalized families can help provide a head start in life. Such efforts can help to mitigate the educational underachievement of children from poor and less literate families. In Singapore society and elsewhere, there is a widening income gap, and there is a population of new poor who are trapped in low-wage jobs contributed to by imported cheap labour, low skills, and poor education. levels. These new poor have both family and social difficulties, which, unless addressed early, can lead to various social consequences which will affect the social health of the community. Volunteers, both young and seniors, can be enlisted by Family Service Centres (FSCs) to collaborate with other community groups with the support of the Ministry of Education (MOE) and Ministry of Family and Social Development (MSF) to initiate early social and educational intervention programmes such as family mentoring, counselling, family life education, educational head start, care networks, income supplement projects, and early reading. Through various educational enrichment endeavours by volunteers, more children in low-income families can be targeted to benefit from early supportive education and literacy programmes. In the longer term, the social divide might be further widened when more low-income children fail to acquire the knowledge and skills that can enable them to earn a competitive wage, thereby reducing the present Gini coefficient of 0.49 (Yearbook of Statistics Singapore, 2017), based on per household member after discounting government transfers. There is much potential for the various public housing estate neighbourhoods to encourage more able Singaporeans to support educational enrichment and early head start programmes to assist the young of less able Singaporeans. Here, one can use Aggregated IT to ensure that most needy children who want a volunteer to mentor them get one. A good match of those who have a need to those who can volunteer their service to meet educational needs can be made. In doing this, voluntary initiatives on a community-wide scale can prevent social fracture within our society and promote social transfer and bonding, demonstrating that there are volunteers who care.

Volunteer involvement in collective fundraising efforts

The establishment of centralized fundraising through the Singapore Community Chest (SCC) was a good move to provide financial resources to the work of charities. This setup reduces the duplication of volunteer drives to raise funds more efficiently, but in the process has inadvertently affected the opportunities for involving more volunteers. Mega-fundraising projects do not tap more volunteers than necessary to run the events, as these are outsourced to event management companies. There is a place for centralized fundraising, but more organizations must encouraged to have a share in the fundraising efforts. When more fundraising projects are decentralized, based on thematic funding appeals, more volunteers could be mobilized to participate. In the long run, volunteers across all societal levels have a part to play in the care and share in fundraising for a few major charitable causes each year. The place for volunteers in fundraising efforts must not be weaned off. The danger faced in due course is when too much emphasis given on centralized fundraising, this will reinforce too much dependency on the CCS. As a consequence the role of volunteers in running appeals for public funding support for various charities will wane. New opportunities for volunteer participation in fundraising for different social and charitable causes can be implemented through many charities, and many volunteers of varied persuasions and social standings, rich and not-so-rich, can play a part in fundraising activities. The view that too many charitable appeals can cause compassion fatigue does not hold; it can in fact prod the social conscience of different sectors of society. Fundraising will also lead to greater public accountability in the utilization of the funds raised from donations.

Conclusion: Future of volunteerism

Volunteer participation and management are critical for the growth and development of the social service sectors, including charities. Volunteer groups and organizations must also encourage beneficiaries to take ownership of the various social and economic activities that are delivered in the various neighbourhoods in partnership with a number of community groups. To have an impact, volunteer groups and organizations cannot continue to assume that they know what beneficiaries or residents want. They all must outreach to appraise their social needs or requirements of the community. In short, community betterment and development should promote self-help, and the focus should be on encouraging mutual help and not dependency and helplessness.

As various regions of the world have become more globalized, social needs and problems have become more challenging to solve, as they require the efforts of a number of key players. Therefore, community problem-solving will require the partnership of several parties and, importantly, a place for volunteers to play a role as well. The partnership model of the government, community organizations and volunteer groups , the corporate sector, and philanthropic individuals can be encouraged to share the social burdens. All partners involved in community problem-solving have shared social responsibilities.

It will be anticipated that in older urban neighbourhoods there will be a demand for care and support for the elderly who live on their own. There will be a lack of young voluntary manpower available for social and welfare agencies to rely on for carrying out such activities, especially when the young will be burdened with work and caring for both their young children and elderly parents. Therefore, it will be prudent to build a reservoir of active seniors who can provide care and attention to the elderly requiring support. As for the emerging younger urban places, there will be younger persons and youth manpower resources, and hence they can be approached to provide help to ageing communities. This scenario will be the case in urban settings where aged burdens will be the issue to address whereas in new developing urban settings there will be surplus younger manpower. So, a social exchange voluntary human service bank can be initiated.

A comprehensive outfit to recruit, deploy flexibly, recognize, train, and develop volunteers for effective and meaningful voluntary social contribution will have a lasting impact on socially healthy communities in Singapore. In the future, volunteer participation and management will be a click away, and Aggregated IT will be used to effectively match volunteers based on their offer of service to those in need of help. This aggregative systems technology will help enhance volunteer participation and management and enable the delivery of services to persons in need of help. Hopefully, a personalized caring and helping services could be given with compassion.

Bibliography[†]

Berger, G., Blugerman, L., Guo, C., Petrov, R., and Smith, D.H. (2016). Relationships and collaboration among associations. In Smith, D.H., Stebbins, R.A., and Grotz, J. (Ed.), *The Palgrave Handbook of Volunteering, Civic Participation, and Non Profit Associations*, pp. 1162–1187. New York: Palgrave Macmillan.

Colomy, P., Chen, H., and Andrew, G.L. (1987). Situational facilities and volunteer work. *The Journal of Volunteer Administration*, 20–25.

Department of Statistics (2014). Population Trend 2014. Singapore.

Esman, M.J. (1978). Development administration and constituency organisation. *Public Administration Review*, 38(2), 166–172.

Gidron, B. (1983). Sources of job satisfaction. *Journal of Voluntary Action*, 12(1), 20–35.

Goh, C.T. (2000). Prime Minister's National Day Rally Speech 2000, pp. 22–25. Singapore Government: Ministry of Information and the Arts.

Goh, L.G., Kua, E.H., and Chiang, H.D. (2015). *Ageing in Singapore: The Next 50 Years*. Singapore: Spring Publishing Ltd.

Lee, K.Y. (2000). *From Third World to First: The Singapore Story, 1965-2000*, pp. 143–157. Singapore: Times Media.

[†]Volunteer participation is defined as efforts either jointly or on their own of Government, corporate sector, community organizations, not-for-profit groups, and/or voluntary welfare organizations (VWOs) to promote community betterment and community problem-solving by involving people based on mutual help or self-help and planned changes. The outcome is community ownership in promoting community well-being.

Nesbit, R., Rimes, H., Smith, D.H., Akhter, S. Akingbola, K., Domaradzka, A., Kristmundsson, O., Malunga, C., and Sasson, U. (2016). Leadership and Management of Associations. In Smith, D.H., Stebbins, R.A., and Grotz, J. (Eds.) *The Palgrave Handbook of Volunteering, Civic Participation, and Non Profit Associations*, pp. 915–949. New York: Palgrave Macmillan.

Olson, M. (1965). *The Logic of Collective Action: Public Goods and the Theory of Groups*. Massachusetts: Harvard University Press.

Rothschild, J., Chen, K.K., and Smith, D.H. (2016). Avoiding bureaucratization and mission drift in associations. In Smith, D.H., Stebbins, R.A., and Grotz, J. (Eds.), *The Palgrave Handbook of Volunteering, Civic Participation, and Non Profit Associations*, pp. 1007–1024. New York: Palgrave Macmillan

Seah, C.M. (1973). *Community Centres in Singapore: Their Political Involvement*. Singapore: Singapore University Press.

Smith, D.H., Never, B., Abu-Rumman, S., Afaq, A.K., Bethmann, S., Gavelin, K., Heitman, J.H., Jaishi, T., Kutty, A.D., Mati, J., Paturyan, Y.J., Petrov, R.G., Pospíšilová, T., Svedberg, L., and Torpe, L. (2016). Scope and trends of volunteering and associations. In Smith, D.H., Stebbins, R.A., and Grotz, J. (Eds.), *The Palgrave Handbook of Volunteering, Civic Participation, and Non Profit Associations*, pp. 1241–1283. New York: Palgrave Macmillan.

Sundblom, D., Smith, D.H., Selle, P., Dansac, C., and Jensen, C. (2016). Life cycles of individual associations. In Smith, D.H., Stebbins, R.A., and Grotz, J. (Eds.), *The Palgrave Handbook of Volunteering, Civic Participation, and Non Profit Associations*, pp. 950–974. New York: Palgrave Macmillan.

Vasoo, S. (1991). Grassroots mobilization and citizen participation: Issues and challenges. *Community Development Journal*, 26(1), 1–7.

Vasoo, S. (1994). *Neighbourhood Leaders Participation in Community Development*. Singapore: Academic Press.

Wiarda, H.J., Adams, P., Lam, W.M., and Wilson, D. (2016). Corporatism vs. pluralism and authoritarianism as association centexts. In Smith, D.H., Stebbins, R.A., and Grotz, J. (Eds.) *The Palgrave Handbook of Volunteering, Civic Participation, and Non Profit Associations*, pp. 1116–1138. New York: Palgrave Macmillan.

Yap, M.T. and Gee, C. (2015). Ageing in Singapore: Social issues and policy challenges. In Chan, D. (Ed.), *50 Years of Social Issues in Singapore*, pp. 3–10. Singapore: World Scientific.

Chapter 6

Strategy and Implementation Success for Non-Profit Organizations in Times of Crisis

Vincent Ng Chee Keong

*School of Social Work and Social Development.,
Singapore University of Social Sciences, Singapore*

Introduction

The emergence of the recent COVID-19 pandemic caused tremendous challenges for Non-Profit Organizations (NPOs) all over the world. During this critical period, NPOs faced both existential and operational struggles. As the world has been preparing for the return of the new normal after COVID-19, I have collated some ideas based on a review of various organizational theories and literature and propose how NPOs can utilize this global disruption as an opportunity for strategic review, and suggested some ways to strengthen the work of organizations to respond to emerging social challenges.

Starting with the Mission

Many NPOs' existence and history can be traced to their mission. In fact, the functions and values of NPOs find their expression in their mission statements. The mission is the principal purpose of the organization and the very reason for its existence. According to Anheier (2005), mission statements help to provide a boundary, serve to motivate staff, volunteers, and members, and are useful in evaluation and orientation. Mission statements can both constrain and enable; they constrain because they set the boundaries of the organization's work, and they help prioritize objectives and tasks.

A mission statement answers some fundamental questions that relate to the NPOs' existence: "Why are we here in the first place?" "What do we stand for?" "Who do we serve?" The mission statement highlights the value base of the organization and provides guidance for the NPO's operations. Bryce (2000) identifies five characteristics of good NPO mission statements:

1. A social contract between the organization (and its members) and society at large that spells out what the organization stands for and what it seeks to achieve; it should state the common values, beliefs, and aspirations of the organization;
2. Permanence in the mission is adopted with a long-term vision in mind that will make frequent mission changes unnecessary;
3. Clarity in its formulation; it should clearly communicate the organization's purpose;
4. Approval where the mission is seen as legitimate and relevant by the board and key constituencies, and in compliance with legal requirements;
5. Proof, meaning that the mission's achievement, or lack thereof, is demonstrable, i.e., it can be examined or monitored with the help of performance and impact measures.

Many NPOs' missions can be traced to their original noble intent and their roots to the community or society to which they belong, as they have a strong sense of attachment to and reflection of their respective community. Hence, NPOs are more likely than for-profit providers to put charitable and community preferences before profitability. A strong mission orientation is a distinguishing characteristic of the non-profit sector. This is a motivating force for many NPOs.

Missions are at the very core of NPOs and provide both an internal and external expression of the goals and values of the organization. Brown and Yoshioka (2003) found that NPO employees who were more attached to the mission of their organization were also more likely to be engaged. In the same vein, employees who were aware and believed in the mission and values, and felt that the programme they worked in supported the mission, were more engaged than those who felt different. This demonstrates the importance of mission not only in guiding organizations but also in creating meaning in the work individuals do on a daily basis.

Missions are Paramount in NPOs

An NPO's vision and mission provide a good starting point for assessing its capacity and needs. On top of the types of programmes and services offered by the NPO, they can also affect the capacity building of the NPO, such as attracting and retaining leadership, recruiting new employees, and raising funds (De Vita *et al.*, 2001). Leaders, prospective employees, and potential donors invariably look for a good match between their own needs, personal goals, aspirations, and values and those promulgated by the NPOs. Similarly, the guiding principles of the vision and mission statement will shape the outreach activities of the organization. Last but not least, the NPO's vision and mission also provide an important context for measuring the effectiveness of its work and existential success.

The NPO's values, mission, and goals form its bedrock because they essentially specify the purpose of the NPO. A clear mission statement from an NPO can impact its performance in two aspects, namely, the internal and external influence. The former impacts the organization's direction and the performance of managers and employees. Clarifying the NPO's purpose is important because different understandings of purpose within an organization can lead to confusion and conflict among those in control.

As for external influence, this covers the NPO's capacity to convey information to external stakeholders. Balser and McClusky (2005) highlighted that for NPOs, the organization's mission statement is very vital for improving their popularity and influencing their perceived effectiveness and legitimacy. Those whose mission statements are unclear and outdated can result in falling support from various stakeholders.

Translating Mission to Strategy

A clear and compelling mission statement can help translate a strategic plan for the entire organization. Alcorn (1998) underscores the importance of the mission by stating that the most important step within the planning process for an NPO is the development of a clear mission. It is followed by a vision statement for the future and then a strategic plan to fulfil both the mission and vision (Adrover and Stalder, 2019).

Having established the NPO's mission statement, it is essential to periodically revisit the mission to ensure that programmes and services remain in line with the identity of the NPO so as to prevent mission drift. According to Bennett and Savani (2011), this is when an NPO's priorities and activities deviate from the organizational mission. As Kaplan (2001) observes, an NPO performing activities that are related to a clear and specific mission statement tends to have higher chances of attaining the impact and its goals.

A good organizational strategy involves developing a coherent set of objectives that can help the NPO create specific and realistic programmes to conduct its mission and set priorities for its goals. Kloppenborg and Laning (2014) assert that converting mission statements into actions is key for organizations' robustness. Hence, planning is crucial for formulating strategies and it is one of the most important aspects of organizational management (Rana *et al.*, 2017).

However, in the context of NPOs, the translation of the mission into actions in different ways that are aligned through a network of volunteers and paid staff is highly challenging. This is unique to NPOs because different personalities and people are attracted to join the NPO because of varying personal and professional affiliations. As such they interpret differently the NPO's mission statement. Kloppenborg and Laning (2014) added that this can be further aggravated if there is a lack of alignment between the NPO's mission and their everyday actions. As such, McHatton *et al.* (2011) stated the increasing relevance of NPO strategic planning will enable the accomplishment of their mission, to meet the needs of their stakeholders and parties of interest.

Strategic Planning in NPOs

There are five models which NPOs can adopt in their strategic planning. They are basic strategic planning, issue-based (or goal-based) planning, the alignment model, scenario planning, and organic (or self-organizing) planning (Kriemadis and Theakou, 2007). As the NPO is formulating its strategy, it has to pay attention to the different stakeholders that are involved and their interests, and to enable alignment with the mission and strategy. In a nutshell, the alignment between environment, mission, strategy, and stakeholder interests contributes to the NPO's success (Adrover and Stalder, 2019).

Research has shown that longer-term planning has been a major weakness of many NPOs (Liket and Maas, 2015). The absence of a long-term vision can cause both a lack of strategic focus and a failure to prioritize their planned activities correctly. On the other hand, in today's dynamic and ever-changing environment, NPOs, having developed a long-term vision, must be willing and ready to continuously review their plans and adapt whenever needed (Allison and Kaye, 2003; Anheier, 1994; Bryson, 2010; Sheehan, 1996). Philbin and Mikush (2012) argue that strategic thinking and planning are integral to the way organizations operate on a daily basis.

Goal setting

The first stage of the planning process is goal setting. This is where goals for achieving the mission and vision of the organization are developed. A goal describes what the NPO must do in order to conduct its mission and achieve its vision. It also constitutes moving from broad organizational goals to specific operational goals, so as to enable immediate measurement of progress and the opportunity to ascertain and document key accomplishments in due course.

The way in which the goals are set out in the strategic plan has an important bearing on its effectiveness (Copps and Vernon, 2010; Kaplan, 2001; Sowa *et al.*, 2004). Successful NPOs tend to assemble detailed goals and objectives, employ future financial projections, allocate relevant resources, reinvest in future growth, and use partnerships strategically and in a sustainable manner. According to Kaplan (2001), quantifying and measuring organizational strategy can prevent ambiguity and confusion about the organizational objectives, goals, and management methods in the NPO. Liket and Maas (2015) thus recommend that setting SMART goals (defined as Specific, Measurable, Attainable, Relevant, and Time-bound) is considered to be the most practical measure of an effective strategic plan.

Alignment

Alignment among the leaders within the NPO regarding the key decisions and actions leading to achieving those SMART goals is crucial for success. NPO leaders must understand their organization's culture and determine how it affects strategy implementation. Some NPOs have strong historical standing. The intimate knowledge and sensitivity of the NPO's heritage and legacy can help leaders effect the necessary changes via the cultural dimension of the organization, so as to ensure alignment for effective implementation of strategy (Lassiter, 2007).

Measurement of success

As soon as the NPO leadership team is aligned on the goals that are set to achieve its strategy, the next important step is to select suitable measures or indicators to track and measure success. These indicators are commonly known as key performance indicators (KPIs). However, many NPOs face challenges when attempting to define and measure success. This is because in some instances, defining and measuring success can be exceedingly difficult conceptually. It is especially so for NPOs whose purpose and mission are related to enhancing normative qualities of the human experience, for example, building a world without barriers, maximizing an individual's potential, destigmatization, social change, and equality. To overcome this common difficulty, NPOs can start by creating amongst its key stakeholders a consensus on how the organization's vision, purpose, strategic goals, and plans are clearly understood. Also priorities and desired outcomes are defined in appropriately and agreed. With greater clarity, the NPO is in a better state to now articulate and measure its performance in executing its intended strategy and mission (Cothran and Clouser, 2009).

Evaluation

Tracking KPIs helps the NPO monitor the progress of its performance of translating strategy into actionable plans. However, an often neglected aspect of strategy implementation is evaluation. Evaluation provides insight into "what has worked, what did not, and why it failed" and "how far off" the NPO is from its strategic goals. Philbin and Mikush (2012) posit that effective organizations periodically take stock of their strengths and weaknesses and the environment in which they work in order to set clear goals, objectives, methods, and tasks. Periodic evaluations aim to clarify which activities are getting results or proving unproductive, which tasks and objectives need to be refined, and how monitoring can take place. Evaluative reports can support NPO leaders in modifying the key processes and goals in a timely manner to enhance good overall performance.

A good and responsible NPO is accountable to its stakeholders, such as service users, funders, its own board, staff members, and even the wider community or society at large (Australia Institute of Company Directors, 2013). Evaluation is valued as a means by the NPOs to enhance their effectiveness and to account for the people they serve. Such NPOs actively evaluate their work, learn from both success and failure, share what they have learned with colleagues in other organizations, and promote best practices. So ultimately, evaluation of any NPO's programme can bring about improvements in sectorial performance, effectiveness, and resource utilization. It strengthens the wider society's aspiration that persons and communities who are needy and vulnerable will be served and supported.

Successful Implementation

Deployment of resources

Having a clearly defined organizational strategy while crucial does not bring about success on its own. Resources are an essential and critical component of the strategy implementation. According to Pfeffer and Salancik (2003), resources are crucial for NPOs' operations. They affect the organization's ability to conduct its mission, attract competent leadership, and accomplish the tasks to meet the desired objectives. Good allocation and assembling of resources can enhance organizational capabilities and create a competitive advantage for an NPO that may not have access to extensive resources (Grant, 1991; Bharadwaj, 2000).

The scarcity of resources is a challenge that NPOs have to manage. Typically for NPOs, resources come in two main forms: financial and human. The former is usually in the form of donation monies, sponsorships, and grants, while the latter consists of paid employees and volunteers. After all, the donor pool is finite and every NPO is competing for the same pie. Many countries in the world are also reducing the burden of social security programmes that fund NPOs. In such an environment, NPO leaders have to prioritize allocating resources to those few capabilities that are most essential to delivering strategic goals (Blenko *et al.*, 2019).

How resources are used is also a critical factor. One effective way of extending resources for use is through training of staff and volunteers, and transforming service users into service contributors. In a rapidly changing environment, upgrading skills and refining current procedures can help stretch limited resources. Human talent is the essential resource that brings about success to the organization (von Eckardstein and Brandl, 2004; Liao and Huang, 2016).

By having the right people to execute and deliver its strategy and objectives at all levels, an organization stands a strong chance to reach its full potential. The most effective NPOs offer strong training and personal and professional development, build a collaborative and cohesive culture, and intentionally inscribe the organization's mission to instil passion in its staff and volunteers (Lamy and Ahktar, 2015; Parsehyan, 2017a).

Applying technology

COVID-19 has brought forward in many NPOs the need to apply technology so as to ensure services are not disrupted. Almost every authority in the world had at one point in time imposed strict "lockdown" or social distancing measures. The conventional ways in which many services were rendered by NPOs were affected. Staff had to work from home and social interactions were stringently curtailed by legislation. Service users could not physically access the services that they needed. In response, many NPOs had to adapt quickly to revamp their established services and procedures in order to deal with the needs of their constituents. Those that could not adapt became irrelevant as resources were channelled to others who were more agile and responsive.

Prior to COVID-19, many programmes and services offered by NPOs depended on face-to-face contact premised on the human touch and interpersonal relationships. COVID-19 forced many NPOs to hasten their digitalization outreach and service provision through remote means. According to a study by Anderson *et al.* (2020), it is now widely accepted by NPOs that the use of technology can improve operational efficiencies, thereby freeing up their limited human resources to focus on mission delivery.

In addition, new information technology (IT) tools and solutions such as Zoom or Microsoft Teams have also been adopted widely by various stakeholders in the NPO care sector, which has resulted in changing service users' behaviours and expectations. Apart from improving operational efficiencies, NPOs are now inclined to push the IT boundary, looking at data collection, integration, and employing data analytics to obtain real-time insights on socio- demographics and health wellness status, to make better informed decisions about service delivery.

According to Hackler and Saxton (2007), organizations which harness the power of IT are more likely to increase their organizational effectiveness. Other studies clearly pointed to the positive impact of IT on developing better organizational partnerships, generating financial stability, or utilizing electronic network communication (Hackler and Saxton, 2007; Burt and Taylor, 2000). NPOs that are unable to effectively employ IT tools will find it hard to remain competitive (Gratton, 2018). Notwithstanding this, NPOs have to approach IT strategically with a plan in order to benefit from these innovations. Otherwise, just having IT alone will not ensure that the NPO mission is accomplished.

Improving work processes

Applying technology to improve overall efficiency must go hand in hand with work process improvements. This contributes to improving consistency and quality-of-service delivery. It is particularly crucial as NPOs often have to manage with tight resources and rising societal expectations. According to Word *et al.* (2011), NPOs must ensure that their programme activities create value, avoid duplication, and streamline work processes. This can greatly supplement the work role clarity for employees, leading to strong alignment with the strategy and improved understanding of their work objectives and goals (Kim *et al.*, 2020). The more employees understand what is expected and required of them, the better they can work toward achieving those goals. Compassion Capital Fund National Resource Centre (n.d.) states that knowing how one fits into and supports the organization facilitates a healthy degree of self-management and peer management, and often results in a more motivated and engaged workforce for the NPO.

Epilogue: Leadership Makes or Breaks an NPO

Strong leadership makes the difference between success and failure in implementing an NPO's programmes and services. In fact, the success of the NPO's performance is highly dependent on leadership (Phipps and

Burbach, 2010). First and foremost, NPO leaders must possess the vision and ability to translate the desired purpose and ideals of the NPO into its mission. This would highlight the commitment and the willingness of the leadership to fulfil the mission. De Vita *et al.* (2001) found that good NPO leaders are those who have a strong sense of ownership in the NPO's work and set standards for organizational performance. Strong and consistent leadership can lead to spillover of the positive impact to other areas of the NPO's development. Having effective leaders helps enhance the NPO's image, prestige, and reputation. Such leaders are instrumental in establishing partnerships, collaborations, and other working relationships that advance the goals of the organization.

Secondly, succession planning in the leadership of the NPOs is fundamental to the sustainability of a good NPO. One of the limitations of NPO leadership is the aura of founder-leaders in many NPOs. Such leaders are often dynamic, charismatic, and highly revered in the NPO by the board, employees, and other stakeholders. Whilst the personal commitment and conviction of founder-leaders are seldom in doubt, there is a risk of the NPO turning into a personality-driven organization. The danger of such an insidious process is the leadership becoming outdated, obsolete, and irrelevant. To mitigate such a risk, the NPO must constantly train new leaders to stimulate and invigorate the work and intentionally groom a new generation of leaders (Parsehyan, 2017b; Storhannus and Larsson, 2008). This process is likely to lead to greater socio-demographic diversity within the leadership ranks of the non-profit sector to better reflect the people and communities that it serves (De Vita *et al.*, 2001).

Good leadership is not only important for an NPO's sustainability but also important for the employees (Parsehyan, 2017b). One of the key responsibilities of leaders is to influence the employees and lead them towards their objectives. This can be achieved through motivating the employees and providing positive role models in the NPO. Puth (2002) identifies several values and principles that NPO leaders must demonstrate in successful NPOs. These include integrity, adaptability, motivational capacity, visionary thinking, diversity learning, people development, and empowerment. Another critical factor in NPO leadership is the leader's ability to articulate and constantly reinforce the mission to employees, in order to bring everyone in the organization on board in pursuit of the mission. Engaged employees are expected to bring positive results to work performance because the experience of engagement is related to one's sense of achievement and positive work experience (Kim *et al.*, 2020; Word *et al.*, 2011).

Last but not least, NPO leaders must learn to effectively navigate and build consensus amongst multiple and diverse stakeholders (Hannum *et al.*, 2011). This can be achieved by strengthening stakeholder engagement, where potentially useful information can be provided to the board, such as how the NPO and its purpose are perceived and possible funding risks or opportunities. Moreover, it improves the NPO's relationships with its stakeholders and increases the likelihood of the NPO attaining its mission (Australia Institute of Company Directors, 2013). In other words, effective NPO leadership is the ability to design a common pursuit and a process through which the vision and objectives of people, groups, or organizations are achieved.

A final acid test: As the whole world re-enters a new phase of normality, NPOs must not be absorbed by present-day issues and challenges. Instead, they must be equipped with a lens for the future. COVID-19 has brought to the fore a hard truth for civic society and with it, a clarion call. It is imperative that NPOs embark on strategic review, resource prioritization, optimization of work operations and processes, and leadership renewal on an urgent basis. For the sake of humanity, NPOs must be better prepared for another black-swan event like COVID-19 and must act in favour of better redistributive justice.

Bibliography

Adrover, M.M. and Stalder, L. (2019). The uniqueness of strategic planning in non-for-profit organizations: A new lens from a stakeholder perspective. Master's Thesis, Linkoping University. http://www.diva-portal.org/smash/get/diva2:1334340/FULLTEXT01.pdf.

Alcorn, M.D. (1998). Building vision in non-profit organizations. http://alcornassociates.com/docsnf/MDAArtVision.pdf.

Allison, M. and Kaye, J. (2003). *Strategic Planning for Non-profit Organizations: A Practical Guide and Workbook*. Hoboken, NJ: John Wiley.

Anderson, M., Dassel, K., Myers, K., and Decker, K.C. (2020). Disruption, resiliency, and improvement: Today's non-profit leaders and how they are addressing COVID-19 and beyond. Deloitte Development LLC. https://www2.deloitte.com/content/dam/Deloitte/us/Documents/public-sector/us-gps-disruptions-resiliency-dealing.pdf.

Anheier, H. (1994). Internationalization of the non-profit sector. In Herman, R.D. and Associates (Eds.), *The Jossey-Bass Handbook of Non-profit Leadership and Management*, pp. 100–116. San Francisco, CA: Jossey-Bass.

Anheier, H.K. (2005). *Non-profit Organizations: Theory, Management, Policy*. Routledge, London. https://citeseerx.ist.psu.edu/viewdoc/download?doi=10. 1.1.452.6420&rep=rep1&type=pdf.

Australian Institute of Company Directors. (2013). Good governance principles and guidance for not-for-profit organisations. https://www.company directors.com.au/~/media/cd2/resources/director-resources/nfp/pdf/nfp-principles-and-guidance-131015.ashx.

Balser, D. and McClusky, J. (2005). Managing stakeholder relationships and non-profit organization effectiveness. *Non-profit Management and Leadership*, 15(3), 295–315.

Bennett, R. and Savani, S. (2011). Surviving mission drift: How charities can turn dependence on government contract funding to their own advantage. *Non-profit Management and Leadership*, 22(2), 217–231.

Bharadwaj, A. (2000). A resource-based perspective on information technology capability and firm performance: An empirical investigation. *Management Information Systems Quarterly*, 24(1), 169–196.

Blenko, M., MacKrell, L., and Rosenberg, K. (2019). Operating models: How non-profits get from strategy to results. The Bridgespan Group. https://www. bridgespan.org/bridgespan/Images/articles/operating-models-nonprofits-strategy-to-results/operating-models-how-nonprofits-get-from-strategy-to-results.pdf.

Brown, W.A. and Yoshioka, C.F. (2003) Mission attachment and satisfaction as factors in employee retention. *Non-profit Management and Leadership*, 14(1), 5–18.

Bryce, H.J. (2000). *Financial and Strategic Management for Non-profit Organizations*. San Francisco, CA: Jossey-Bass.

Bryson, J.M. (2010). Strategic planning and the strategy change cycle. In Renz, D.O. and Herman, R.D. (Eds.), *The Jossey-Bass Handbook of Non-profit Management and Leadership*, 3rd edn., pp. 230–261. San Francisco, CA: John Wiley.

Burt, E. and Taylor, J.A. (2000). Information and communication technologies: Reshaping voluntary organizations? *Non-profit Management & Leadership*, 11(2), 131–143. DOI: 10.1002/nml.11201.

Compassion Capital Fund National Resource Center. (n.d.). Leading a non-profit organization: Tips and tools for executive directors and team leaders. https:// nonprofitoregon.org/sites/default/files/uploads/file/Leading%20a%20 Nonprofit%20Organization%20-%20Tips%20and%20Tools%20for%20 EDs%20and%20Team%20Leaders%20-%20Strengthening%20Nonprofits%20 %28Guide%29.pdf.

Copps, J. and Vernon, B. (2010). *The Little Blue Book: NPC's Guide to Analysing Charities, for Charities and Funders*. London, England: New Philanthropy Capital.

Cothran, H. and Clouser, R. (2009). Strategic planning for communities, non-profit organizations, and public agencies. https://www.csus.edu/indiv/s/shulockn/executive%20fellows%20pdf%20readings/u%20fl%20strategic%20planning.pdf.

De Vita, C., Fleming, C., and Twombly, E.C. (2001). Building non-profit capacity, a framework for addressing the problem. In De Vita, C., Fleming, C., and Twombly, E. (Eds.), *Building capacity in Non-profit Organisations*. The Urban Institute. http://research.urban.org/UploadedPDF/building_capacity.PDF.

von Eckardstein, D. and Brandl, J. (2004). Human resource management in non-profit organizations. In Zimmer, A. and Priller, E. (Eds.), *Future of Civil Society*. Wiesbaden: VS Verlag für Sozialwissenschaften. DOI: 10.1007/978-3-322-80980-3_17.

Grant, R.M. (1991). The resource-based theory of competitive advantage. *California Management Review*, 33(3), 114–135.

Gratton, P.C. (2018). Organization development and strategic planning for non-profit organizations. *Organization Development Journal*, 36(2), 27–38.

Hackler, D. and Saxton, G.D. (2007). The strategic use of information technology by non-profit organizations: Increasing capacity and untapped potential. *Public Administration Review*, 67(3), 474–487. DOI: 10.1111/j.1540-6210.2007.00730.x.

Hannum, K.M., Deal, J., Howard, L.L., Lu, L.S., Ruderman, M.N., Stawiski, S., Zane, N., and Price, R. (2011). *Emerging Leadership in Non-profit Organizations: Myths, Meaning, and Motivations*. Greensboro, NC: Center for Creative Leadership.

Kaplan, R. (2001). Strategic performance measurement and management in non-profit organizations. *Non-profit Management & Leadership*, 11, 353–370.

Kim, J., Kim, H., and Kwon, H. (2020). The impact of employees' perceptions of strategic alignment on sustainability: An empirical investigation of Korean firms. *Sustainability*, 12(10), 4180. DOI: 10.3390/su12104180.

Kloppenborg, T. and Laning, L. (2014). *Achieving Success in Non-profit Organizations*, 1st edn. New York: Business Expert Press.

Kriemadis, T. and Theakou, E. (2007). Strategic planning models in public and non-profit sport organizations. *Sport Management International Journal*, 3(2), 27–37.

Lamy, S. and Akhtar, U. (2015). Unlocking the power of Singapore's non-profits. Bain & Company. https://cityofgood.sg/wp-content/uploads/2021/09/Unlocking-The-power-of-Singapores-Nonprofits.pdf.

Lassiter, V.C. (2007). The role of process improvements in the non-profit organization. Master Thesis, University of Pennsylvania. https://repository.upenn.edu/od_theses_msod/5.

Liao, K. and Huang, I. (2016). Impact of vision, strategy, and human resource on non-profit organization service performance. *Procedia - Social and Behavioral Sciences*, 224, 20–27.

Liket, K.C. and Maas, K. (2015). Non-profit organizational effectiveness: Analysis of best practices. *Non-profit and Voluntary Sector Quarterly*, 44(2), 268–296. https://doi.org/10.1177/0899764013510064.

McHatton, P.A., Bradshaw, W., Gallagher, P.A., and Reeves, R. (2011). Results from a strategic planning process: Benefits for a non-profit organization. *Non-profit Management and Leadership*, 22(2), 233–249.

Parsehyan, B.G. (2017a). Human resources management in non-profit organizations: A case study of Istanbul foundation for culture and arts. In Mura, L. (Ed.), *Issues of Human Resource Management*. DOI: 10.5772/intechopen.68816.

Parsehyan, B.G. (2017b). Leadership in non-profit organisations. In Alvinius, A. (Ed.), *Contemporary Leadership Challenges*. DOI: 10.5772/65268.

Pfeffer, J. and Salancik, G.R. (2003). *The External Control of Organizations: A Resource Dependence Perspective*. Stanford: Stanford University.

Philbin, A. and Mikush, S. (2012). A framework for organizational development: The why, what & how. Mary Reynolds Babcock Foundation. https://www.mrbf.org/sites/default/files/organizationaldevelopment.pdf.

Phipps, K.A. and Burbach, M.E. (2010). Strategic leadership in the non-profit sector: Opportunities for research. *Journal of Behavioral and Applied Management*, 11, 137–154.

Puth, G. (2002). *The Communicating Leader: The Key to Strategic Alignment*, 2nd edn. Pretoria: Van Schaik.

Rana, R., Rana F., and Rana, H. (2017). Strategic planning role in non-profit organizations. *Journal for Studies in Management and Planning*, 3, 166–170.

Sheehan, R.R.M. (1996). Mission accomplishment as philanthropic organization effectiveness: Key findings from the excellence in philanthropy program. *Non-profit and Voluntary Sector Quarterly*, 25, 110–123.

Sowa, J., Selden, S., and Sandfort, J. (2004). No longer unmeasurable? A multidimensional integrated model of non-profit organisational effectiveness. *Non-profit and Voluntary Sector Quarterly*, 33, 711–728.

Storhannus, P. and Larsson, L. (2008). Understanding leadership in successful non-profit organizations: A case-study of IKSU. Bachelor Thesis. https://www.diva-portal.org/smash/get/diva2:141329/FULLTEXT01.pdf.

Word, J., Norton, L., Davis, S., and Nguyen, A. (2011). Engaging the non-profit workforce. Opportunity Knocks. https://www.gcn.org/sites/default/files/ctools/OK_Engaging_the_Nonprofit_Workforce_Report.pdf.

Chapter 7

Conclusion: Stewardship in Management of Non-Profit Organizations

S. Vasoo

Department of Social Work, National University of Singapore, Singapore

There is an increasing need for people in charge of the non-profit sector to pay more attention to bringing more talented volunteers with management expertise to rejuvenate the moribund state of their organizations. More often than not, there is much resistance to taking positive steps to introduce change as there are hang-ups about displacing office-holders, who have put in many years in their respective set-ups, and incurring painful decisions to replace them. Those in positions of influence must take a proactive approach to decently counsel those needing to be retired so that a renewed management expert can assume leadership. As I note, there are often many people on the boards of management in the non-profit sector who are reluctant to undertake the unpleasant tasks of retiring people who have been loyally associated with the cause but have less drive to undertake tasks which will help their organizations meet new social and economic challenges to survive. There are few key issues that the boards of management must address so that their organizations are more viable and sustainable.

Some Issues

First, the increasing moves to outsource community activities and services can make non-profit organizations insular after which they can become task or activity-centered and eventually they can slowly move away from being people-centered which is aimed at promoting self-help and community ownership. Hence, many non-profit organizations and groups have adopted a non-outreach approach to understand the changing needs of the community. In the longer term, such a move will make them more detached from the understanding needs of people who are uninvolved or are functioning in the margins of livelihoods.

Second, the leadership of non-profit organizations is greying. More attention should be devoted to enlisting resourceful younger residents to help manage them. Many non-profit organizations have become gerontocratic and can be less responsive to the changing needs of the neighbourhoods. Consequently, they can become senior citizen clubs, which will only meet the needs of one specific group of the resident population, namely, the elderly. So far, punctuated attempts have been made to renew leadership and as such, it has not worked.

Third, it is observed that the rate of participation of lower-income households and minorities is not as significant, and this could be due to the less tangible benefits offered by the programmes delivered by non-profit organizations and community groups. The participation of both minorities and lower-income families is critical in maintaining social cohesion and community bonding. Hence, more concrete services should be provided to meet their social and economic needs. This will address the public goods dilemma, as this will reduce their cost of participation. When non-profit organizations do not bear in mind this matter in their service delivery, both minorities and low-income households will not be motivated to participate in some mainstream community activities.

Fourth, another significant development in the older neighbourhoods of Singapore is the hollowing out of the more resourceful and younger residents. When this process accelerates, these neighbourhoods will eventually become silver communities. A higher outflow of young people who are attracted by the exuberant facilities of other New Towns also compounds this. It is anticipated that there will be a depletion of community and leadership resources in these neighbourhoods. This will inevitably slow down and become less attractive to new residents. Inevitably, social burdens for care will increase unless more community care services and support networks are encouraged through community development efforts.

Meeting the Challenges

Some challenges confronting community development in Singapore have been identified. It is therefore appropriate to discuss a few ideas to deal with these challenges. Policymakers, community leaders, and social workers may consider undertaking to enhance community development efforts in the context of Singapore. In enhancing self-help and community ownership, there should be fewer outsourcing contracts and more in-sourcing activities by mobilizing residents to participate in non-profit organizations or social enterprises. Such attempts will provide more opportunities for residents to participate in decision-making so that they can take ownership.

More community care groups and support networks can be established. This will encourage participants to not be passive recipients of services and be engaged in problem-solving. Non-profit organizations need to widen the base of participation by residents by forming various interest groups or task forces to work on various social issues and projects such as security watch and crime prevention, co-operative care services, improvements to recreational facilities, pollution control, thrift and loan societies, micro credit groups, and environmental enhancement projects. It will be useful to encourage residents to take charge of finding more effective ways to deal with local matters.

In this case, the support of the Town Councils (TCs) and Community Development Councils (CDCs) will be helpful. Through this, residents will learn and find more realistic solutions to solve their specific needs and problems and become accountable for their decisions. However, with the move towards information technology, more people could become impersonal and homebound, social interactions could be reduced, and social bonding could be threatened. Therefore, personalized outreach efforts can be conducted with online contacts.

Leadership Rejuvenation and Organizational Renewal

It is observed that a significant number of grassroots leaders of non-profit organizations in mature housing estates are above 50 years old. These organizations face difficulties in recruiting younger residents to assume leadership (Vasoo, 1994, 2002).

With the greying of the organizational leadership, there is an urgency to rejuvenate the leadership of community organizations by attracting younger professionals to participate. It is not just sufficient to recruit them; some committed older leaders must mentor them. With attachment to specific mentors, they can be better affiliated with the organizations, and this will reduce the attrition of younger persons taking up leadership in organizations dominated by seniors. A rejuvenated leadership will continue to be vibrant and relevant to meet the needs and aspirations of the younger generation of residents.

We must also attract younger people to become community leaders and they should be given all the support to conduct community problem-solving activities. People-centered community or organizational leaders are usually proactive. They should not be burdened with so many tasks as this can make them suffer from burnout. More importantly, young leaders should be given management skills training so that they can understand the needs of residents or end users. This can help make non-profit organizations responsive to tackling emerging social needs provided there is an versatile group of leaders with visionary perspectives.

Bibliography

Vasoo, S. (1994). *Neighbourhood Leaders Participation in Community Development*. Singapore: Academic Press.

Vasoo, S. (2019). Community development in Singapore; Issues and challenges. In Vasoo, S. and Singh, B. (Eds.), *Community Development Arenas in Singapore*. Singapore: World Scientific Publishers.

Vasoo, S. (2002). *New Directions in Community Development in Extending Frontiers*. Singapore: Eastern University Press, pp. 20–36.

Vasoo, S. and Singh, B. (2016). *Community Development Arenas in Singapore*. Singapore: World Scientific Publishing Co. Pte. Ltd.

Author Index

Subject Index

www.ingramcontent.com/pod-product-compliance
Lightning Source LLC
Chambersburg PA
CBHW070757300326
41914CB00053B/711